Fortress · 32

OSPREY
PUBLISHING

# Crusader Castles in the Holy Land 1192–1302

David Nicolle · Illustrated by Adam Hook

Series editors Marcus Cowper and Nikolai Bogdanovic

First published in 2005 by Osprey Publishing
Midland House, West Way, Botley, Oxford OX2 0PH, UK
443 Park Avenue South, New York, NY 10016, USA
E-mail: info@ospreypublishing.com

ISBN 1 84176 827 8

Design: Ken Vail Graphic Design, Cambridge, UK
Index by Bob Munro
Originated by PPS Grasmere Ltd, Leeds, UK
Printed and bound in China through Bookbuilders

05 06 07 08 09   10 9 8 7 6 5 4 3 2 1

A CIP catalogue record for this book is available from the British Library.

FOR A CATALOGUE OF ALL BOOKS PUBLISHED BY OSPREY MILITARY AND AVIATION
PLEASE CONTACT:

NORTH AMERICA
Osprey Direct, 2427 Bond Street, University Park, IL 60466, USA
E-mail: info@ospreydirectusa.com

ALL OTHER REGIONS
Osprey Direct UK, P.O. Box 140, Wellingborough, Northants, NN8 2FA, UK
E-mail: info@ospreydirect.co.uk

www.ospreypublishing.com

## Artist's note

Readers may care to note that the original paintings from which
the colour plates in this book, and the preceding volume Fortress
21: *Crusader Castles in the Holy Land 1097–1192*, were prepared are
available for private sale. All reproduction copyright is retained by
the Publishers. All enquiries should be addressed to:

Scorpio Gallery, PO Box 75, Hailsham, East Sussex, BN27 2SL, UK.

The Publishers regret that they can enter into no correspondence
upon this matter.

## Image credits

Unless otherwise indicated, the photographic images and line
drawings that appear in this work are from the author's
collection.

## Dedication

For Selina, because castles could also be places of beauty and
pleasure.

## Measurements

Distances, ranges, and dimensions are given in metric. To covert
these figures to Imperial measures, the following conversion
formulas are provided:

| | |
|---|---|
| 1 millimetre (mm) | 0.0394 in. |
| 1 centimetre (cm) | 0.3937 in. |
| 1 metre (m) | 1.0936 yards |
| 1 kilometre (km) | 0.6214 miles |
| 1 gram (g) | 0.0353 ounces |
| 1 kilogram (kg) | 2.2046 lb |
| 1 tonne (t) | 0.9842 long ton (UK) |

## The Fortress Study Group (FSG)

The object of the FSG is to advance the education of the public in
the study of all aspects of fortifications and their armaments,
especially works constructed to mount or resist artillery. The FSG
holds an annual conference in September over a long weekend
with visits and evening lectures, an annual tour abroad lasting
about eight days, and an annual Members' Day.
The FSG journal *FORT* is published annually, and its newsletter
Casemate is published three times a year. Membership is
international. For further details, please contact:
The Secretary, c/o 6 Lanark Place, London W9 1BS, UK

# Contents

# Introduction

Crusader castles served several purposes at the same time, operating as offensive bases, as defensive bastions, and as statements of power. Which of these roles was the most important may never be answered. The priorities of those who financed, built, garrisoned and defended them changed according to circumstances. At the turn of the 13th century, one thing was, however, clear to the rulers, churchmen, knights, common soldiers and civilians that inhabited them. Since the fiasco of the Second Crusade in 1148 the Crusader States largely had to rely upon their own resources and on diplomatic as well as military methods of defence. Yet this was far from easy. Following the death of the sympathetic Byzantine Emperor Manuel in 1180, it proved impossible for the Crusader States to form a genuine alliance with the Byzantine Empire. In fact increasing diplomatic, political, economic and religious friction between the Orthodox Christian east and the Latin or Catholic west led to a virtual alliance between the Byzantines and the Crusader States' most formidable foe, Saladin.

Consequently the Crusader States developed a more cautious strategy. The original expansionist spirit largely disappeared and was replaced by a pragmatic emphasis on survival within a predominantly hostile environment. Paradoxically, however, there was a decline in cooperation between the remaining three Crusader States as each concentrated on its own immediate problems.

The Third Crusade was at best only a partial success; nevertheless, it achieved more than any subsequent Crusading expeditions. Meanwhile the strengthening of those fortifications that remained in Crusader hands, the building of some new castles, and massive efforts to strengthen the defences of Crusader-held towns, continued until the final collapse in 1291. In some ways the military situation was now easier, because the Latin or western European colonists held fewer positions than they had before the disasters of 1187. Several of these fortified sites were immensely strong, and remain impressive pieces of architecture to this day.

Although the abundance of Crusader castles was a sign of the military weakness of the Crusader States, the popular view that the ruling elites and knights of the 13th-century Crusader States had 'gone soft' as a result of contact with a supposedly enervating Arab-Islamic culture is nonsense. In reality the states of Antioch, Tripoli and Jerusalem (so-called in name only, since the Kingdom of Jerusalem rarely controlled the Holy City itself) had developed effective defensive systems. These were based upon experience, realism and an ability to learn from their neighbours. The baronial families of the Crusader States may have regarded France as their cultural ideal, but in international politics as well as everyday life the elites of the Crusader States had more in common with the urbanised and mercantile elites of 13th-century Italy.

Urbanisation was also a feature of the 13th-century Crusader States. They were now little more than coastal enclaves clinging to the fringe of the Middle East. Of the towns and cities that at various times formed the Kingdom of Jerusalem, only 14 towns had circuit walls. Of these, 12 were already walled before the Crusaders arrived. The two exceptions were Atlit, south of Haifa, which was a new Crusader foundation, and Acre's similarly new suburb of Montmussard. Elsewhere the Crusaders strengthened what already existed, and most of such efforts date from after the Third Crusade. Furthermore, the vast costs of urban refortification projects were often covered by Crusader leaders from western Europe.

Although the Crusader States never recovered from Saladin's campaigns, they did enjoy a limited respite during the rest of the Ayyubid period, when Saladin's successors adopted a less aggressive policy towards the European settlers. A system of fluctuating alliances often characterised this period, with one or more Crusader States allying themselves with one or more of the fragmented Ayyubid sultanates. This impacted upon the history of specific castles, like Belfort, which was lost to Saladin. It was then strengthened by his Ayyubid successors before the Sultan of Damascus agreed to hand it back to the Crusaders as part of an alliance agreement in 1240. However, the garrison disagreed, and so the Sultan had to besiege his own fortress in order to hand it over to the Christians. The titular lord of Belfort then died and his successor sold the castle to the Templars, because this wealthy Military Order was better able to defend it. During the few years that the Templars held Belfort they were credited with constructing an outwork, 250m from the main castle, to stop a besieger dominating the fortress from a nearby hill, probably reflecting the increasing range of stone-throwing siege machines.

These years also saw some 'offensive' building projects, perhaps including work on a new citadel in Tiberius, though there is no evidence that the town was recolonised. Even Jerusalem was regained by negotiation in 1229, only to be lost permanently 15 years later. During this brief reoccupation, efforts were made to strengthen the fortifications that had been rased by Saladin, including work on two gates. However, this cannot have been effective, as even local Muslim peasants could sometimes break in.

The situation became far more serious during the second half of the 13th century, when the warlike Mamluk Sultanate replaced the Ayyubids. This period saw major efforts to strengthen Crusader defences, especially urban fortifications. The castles, which had proved quite successful during the first half of the 13th century, were now picked off as part of a Mamluk grand strategy initiated by Sultan Baybars. The Christians responded with even stronger fortifications and a massive building programme during the final decades of the Crusader States.

By 1242 changes in the balance of power between the king and his barons resulted in new laws regarding the custody of royal fortresses. Meanwhile other fortifications were appearing within some Crusader-held coastal cities. Here virtually autonomous Italian merchant communes were playing an increasingly important military and political role, while also importing their own quarrels – rivalries that led to Genoese, Venetians and Pisans attacking each others' fortified towers inside cities such as Acre. Similarly the rivalry between 'Imperial' and 'anti-Imperial' factions for domination of what remained of the Kingdom of Jerusalem not only caused brawling in the streets but even small-scale siege warfare. Given such mounting problems, it is not surprising that much of the Crusader aristocracy abandoned Syria, Lebanon and Palestine to seek new opportunities in Crusader-ruled Cyprus and the Crusader States of Greece (the subject of a third Fortress volume in this sequence, *Crusader Castles in Cyprus, Greece and the Aegean 1191–1571*).

Despite the vulnerable situation in which the Crusader States found themselves, many 13th-century fortifications seem to have been built for offensive as well as defensive purposes. Furthermore, it is wrong to suggest that the Crusader States now had no broad military strategy. Another entrenched myth maintains that Crusader fortifications formed a 'Line of Defence'. In fact they continued to serve as secure centres of administration while providing bases for both offence and defence. Furthermore these castles, fortified towns, cities and even isolated towers could support one another to some extent. Their functions, and the military thinking that lay behind them, were essentially the same in the 13th century as they had been in the 12th. Their eventual failure resulted from the unification of Egypt and Syria under the aggressive leadership of the Mamluk sultans – just as the catastrophe of 1187–88 resulted from the

**The aftermath of catastrophe**

Saladin's victory over the army of the Crusader States at Hattin in 1187 was followed by Islam regaining Jerusalem and almost all of what had been the Kingdom of Jerusalem. The County of Tripoli also lost territory although the Principality of Antioch suffered far less. A fourth Crusader state, the County of Edessa, had already fallen to Islamic reconquest. These events were the immediate background to the Third Crusade, which then became a massive effort led by three senior Western European rulers to regain what had been lost. The effort failed, but it enabled the Crusader States to survive for a further century.

Fortifications of the Crusader States
of the Middle East, c. 1241, and the
main areas controlled by the
Military Orders.

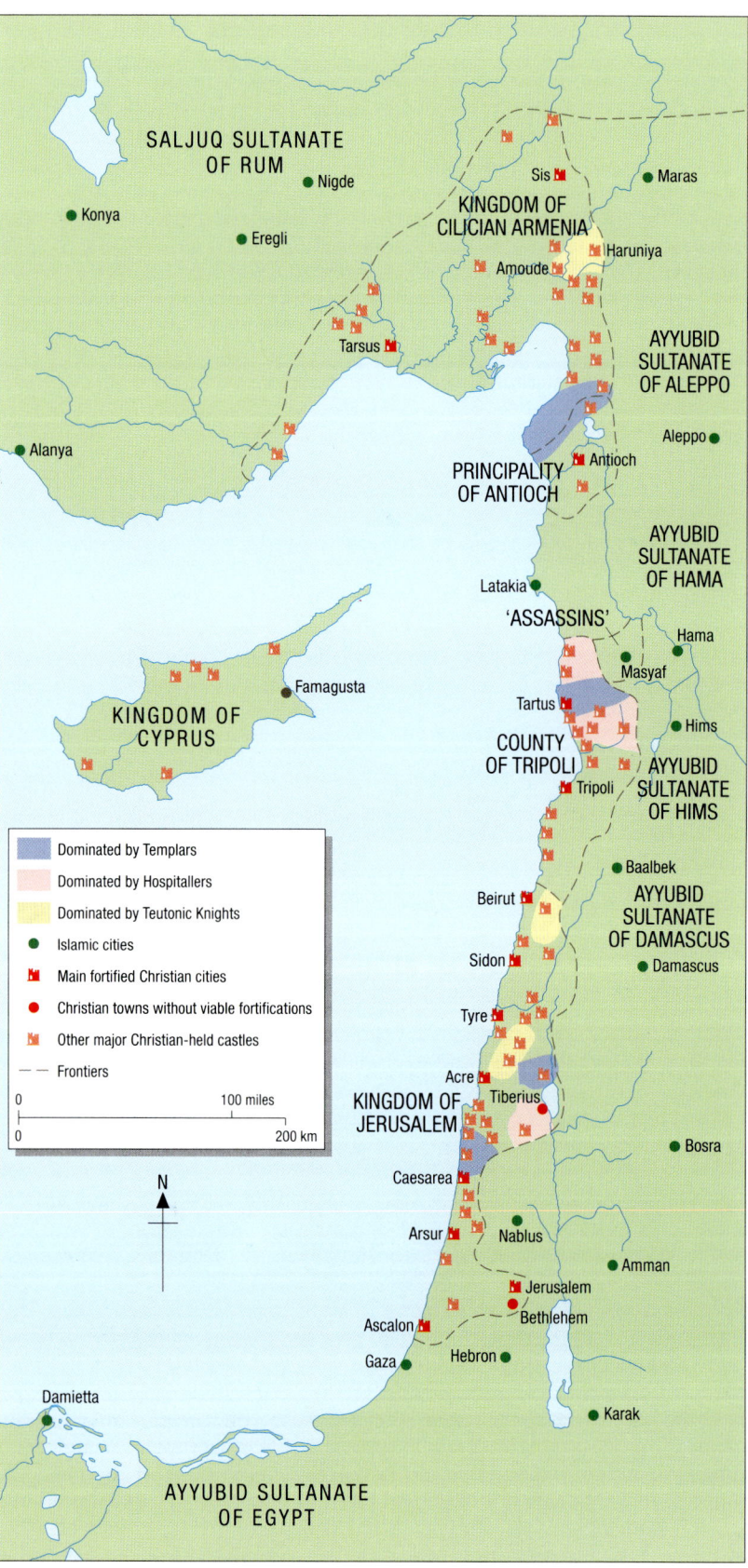

SALJUQ SULTANATE
OF RUM

● Nigde
● Maras
● Sis
KINGDOM OF
CILICIAN ARMENIA
Haruniya
● Konya
Amoude
● Eregli
AYYUBID
SULTANATE
OF ALEPPO
Tarsus
● Alanya
Aleppo ●
Antioch
PRINCIPALITY
OF ANTIOCH
AYYUBID
SULTANATE
OF HAMA
Latakia ●
'ASSASSINS'
Hama ●
Masyaf ●
Tartus
Hims ●
COUNTY
OF TRIPOLI
AYYUBID
SULTANATE
OF HIMS
KINGDOM OF
CYPRUS
Famagusta
Tripoli
● Baalbek
AYYUBID
SULTANATE
OF DAMASCUS
Beirut
Sidon
Damascus ●
Tyre
Acre
Tiberius ●
KINGDOM OF
JERUSALEM
● Bosra
Caesarea
Arsur
Nablus ●
● Amman
Jerusalem
Ascalon
Bethlehem ●
Gaza ●
Hebron ●
● Karak
Damietta
AYYUBID SULTANATE
OF EGYPT

| | Dominated by Templars |
| --- | --- |
| | Dominated by Hospitallers |
| | Dominated by Teutonic Knights |
| ● | Islamic cities |
| | Main fortified Christian cities |
| ● | Christian towns without viable fortifications |
| | Other major Christian-held castles |
| - - | Frontiers |

0                    100 miles
0                    200 km

N

KINGDOM OF CILICIAN ARMENIA
Gökvelioglu
Ayas
Calamella
Payas
Mancilik
Roche
Guillaume
Alexandretta
Chilvan
Kale
Arsuz
Trapesac
Bagra
PRINCIPALITY
OF ANTIOCH
Antioch
AYYUBID
SULTANATE
OF ALEPPO
Cursat
St Simeon
N
Latakia
Balatonos
Jabala
Qal'at al-Mudiq
(Apamea)
Belda
Shayzar
ISMA'ILI
AMIRATE
(ASSASSINS)
Marqab
Maraclea
Masyaf
AYYUBID
SULTANATE
OF HAMA
COUNTY
OF TRIPOLI
Tartus
Principality of Antioch
Other Christian territory
Main fortified Christian cities
Other major Christian-held castles
Christian towns without viable fortifications
Islamic cities
Frontiers
Main routes
0
25 miles
0
50 km

Fortifications of the Principality of Antioch *c.* 1229, and the main communication routes.

unification of Egypt and Syria under Saladin. By the later 13th century, however, the balance of power had shifted strongly in favour of the Muslims, while interest in Crusading and in the fate of the Crusader States slumped in western Europe.

Only one significant inland castle was regained in the Kingdom of Jerusalem, namely Calansue, which was held from 1191 to 1265; the settler population was now even more concentrated on the coast than it had been before 1187. For example, the suburb of Montmussard on the northern side of Acre expanded and required fortification. Jaffa had expanded beyond its pre-Crusader walls, while the new castle at Atlit was soon followed by a new town. A comparable process may have taken place further north, around some of the remaining inland castles like Montfort, Safad and Crac des Chevaliers. Trade was another stimulus to fortification, with small castles protecting vulnerable routes through Crusader territory. Here they could levy tolls, as did the isolated Burj al-Sabi tower, next to the coastal road south of Banyas. Meanwhile fortified towns continued to develop as centres of trade because of the security they offered.

The Principality of Antioch had long been involved in the affairs of the Kingdom of Lesser Armenia in neighbouring Cilicia. During the 13th century the Military Orders were also given several castles in this region. Some were existing Byzantine or Islamic structures, which the Orders strengthened or rebuilt. Others were new foundations. Generally speaking the Armenians only permitted the Crusading Orders to hold castles in the vulnerable south-eastern and south-western border regions, though the Teutonic Knights did play a political role in support of Armenian rulers, perhaps because they were less of a threat than the longer established Hospitallers and Templars.

# Chronology

| | |
|---|---|
| 1189–92 | The Third Crusade sets off for the Middle East; King Richard I of England seizes Cyprus from the Byzantine Empire; Crusaders retake Acre and defeat Saladin at the battle of Arsuf; Crusaders fail to reach Jerusalem; King Richard agrees a peace treaty with Saladin. |
| 1193 | Death of Saladin. |
| 1197 | King Aimery of Cyprus (since 1194) becomes King of Jerusalem (until 1205); German Crusade to the Middle East. |
| 1198 | Cilician Armenia becomes a kingdom; German Hospital reconstituted as the Order of Teutonic Knights. |
| 1202–04 | Fourth Crusade seizes the Byzantine Imperial capital; creation of the Latin Empire of Constantinople; beginning of the Crusader conquest of southern Greece. |
| 1205 | Hugh I becomes king of Cyprus (until 1218). |
| 1210 | John of Brienne becomes King of Jerusalem (until 1225). |
| 1218 | Henry I becomes king of Cyprus (until 1253); Fifth Crusade invades Egypt by sea. |
| 1221 | Fifth Crusade is defeated at the First Battle of Mansurah. |
| 1225 | Emperor Frederick II of Germany and Italy becomes ruler of the Kingdom of Jerusalem (until 1243). |
| 1229 | Civil war in the Kingdom of Cyprus (until 1233). |
| 1231–42 | Commune of Acre becomes centre of resistance to Emperor Frederick II's rule in the Kingdom of Jerusalem. |

The castle of Gaston (Baghras) dominated the strategic Belen Pass through the Amanus Mountains east of Antioch. It consisted of outer and inner circuit walls, both with rounded towers, perched on a very steep hill. After falling to Saladin it passed into the hands of the Armenians, before being returned to the Templars in 1216. Ironically, its most important subsequent role was to protect the Principality of Antioch against its fellow Christian neighbour in the Kingdom of Cilician Armenia.

Fortifications of the County
of Tripoli c. 1229, and the main
communication routes.

**County of Tripoli**
*Other Christian territory*
■ Main fortified Christian cities
■ Main Christian-held castles
● Islamic cities
- - - Frontiers
—— Main routes

0        25 miles
0        50 km

N

PRINCIPALITY
OF ANTIOCH

AYYUBID
SULTANATE
OF HAMA

Jabala

Belda

Marqab

Maraclea

Shayzar

ISMA'ILI
AMIRATE
(ASSASSINS)

Masyaf

Hama

Arwad
Castel Rouge

Tartus
Castel Blanc

Crac des
Chevaliers

Arima

Hims

Halba

Coliat

Villejargon

Gebelcar

Nephin

Tripoli

AYYUBID
SULTANATE
OF HIMS

Botron

Baalbek

Gibelet

Beirut

Sidon

Cave de Tyron

Damascus

Belfort

AYYUBID SULTANATE
OF DAMASCUS

Tor de l'Hopital

KINGDOM OF
JERUSALEM

Tyre

Toron

Castel Neuf

Scandelion

| 1243 | Conrad becomes King of Jerusalem (until 1254); Mongols invade Seljuk Anatolia. |
|---|---|
| 1244 | Kingdom of Jerusalem forms an alliance with the Ayyubid rulers of Damascus and Jordan against the Ayyubid ruler of Egypt; Khwarazian refugee army from eastern Islam (fleeing advancing Mongols) takes Jerusalem from the Crusader Kingdom; Crusader States defeated at the battle of La Forbie. |
| 1245 | Emperor Frederick II deposed. |
| 1250 | Crusade of King Louis IX of France invades Egypt; death of Sultan al-Salih Ayub of Egypt; Louis IX defeated at the Second Battle of Mansurah; effective establishment of the Mamluk Sultanate in Egypt. |
| 1253 | Hugh II becomes King of Cyprus (until 1267). |
| 1254 | Conraddin becomes King of Jerusalem (until 1268; note that Acre was now actual capital of the Kingdom). |

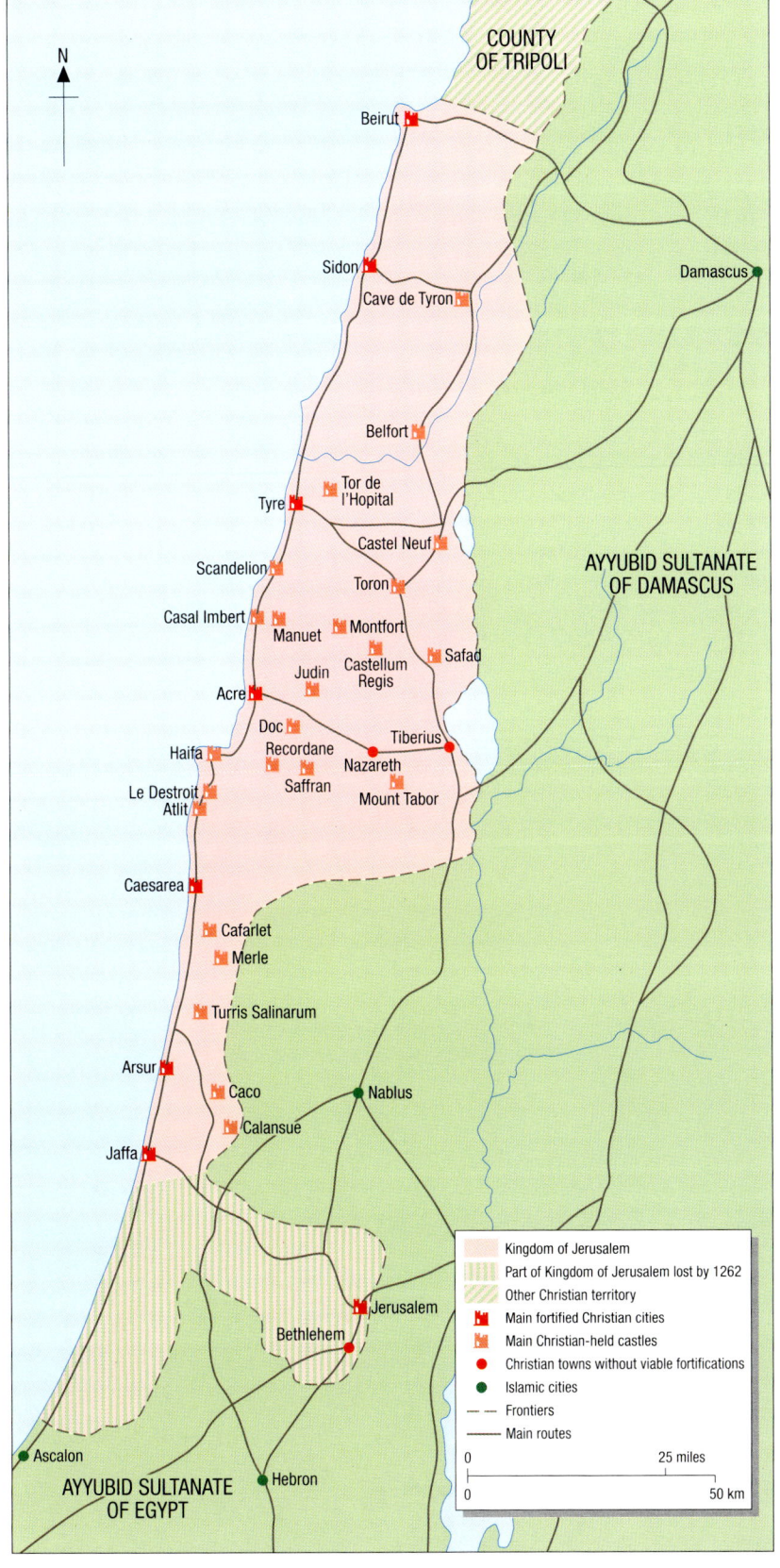

Fortifications of the Kingdom of Jerusalem from 1260 to 1290, and the main communication routes.

**COUNTY OF TRIPOLI**

Beirut

Sidon
Cave de Tyron

Damascus

Belfort

Tor de l'Hopital
Tyre
Castel Neuf

**AYYUBID SULTANATE OF DAMASCUS**

Scandelion
Toron
Casal Imbert
Manuet    Montfort
Judin    Castellum Regis    Safad
Acre
Doc    Tiberius
Recordane    Nazareth
Haifa
Saffran
Le Destroit    Mount Tabor
Atlit

Caesarea

Cafarlet
Merle

Turris Salinarum

Arsur
Caco    Nablus
Calansue
Jaffa

Kingdom of Jerusalem
Part of Kingdom of Jerusalem lost by 1262
Other Christian territory
Main fortified Christian cities
Main Christian-held castles
Christian towns without viable fortifications
Islamic cities
Frontiers
Main routes

Jerusalem
Bethlehem

0    25 miles
0    50 km

Ascalon

**AYYUBID SULTANATE OF EGYPT**
Hebron

11

| | |
|---|---|
| **1256** | Civil war in Acre (until 1258). |
| **1258** | Mongols invade Iraq and sack Baghdad. |
| **1260** | Mongols invade Syria; Crusader Principality of Antioch and Kingdom of Cilician Armenia ally with the Mongols; Mamluks defeat Mongols at the battle of Ayn Jalut; Baybars becomes Mamluk Sultan of Egypt. |
| **1261** | Byzantine Emperor Michael VIII retakes Constantinople from Latin (Crusader) Empire. |
| **1263–66** | Mamluks destroy Nazareth, and take Caesarea, Arsuf and Safad. |
| **1267** | Hugh III becomes King of Cyprus (until 1284). |
| **1268** | Mamluks retake Jaffa, Belfort and Antioch. |
| **1269** | King Hugh III of Cyprus becomes ruler of the Kingdom of Jerusalem (until 1284); Aragonese Crusade arrives in Acre. |
| **1271** | Mamluks retake Castel Blanc, Crac des Chevaliers and Montfort; Crusade of Prince Edward of England reaches Acre then attacks Caco. |
| **1276–77** | King Hugh III abandons Palestine for Cyprus; Mary of Antioch sells the Crown to King Charles of southern Italy; Kingdom of Jerusalem divided between lords who recognise or reject Charles. |
| **1277** | Civil war in the County of Tripoli (until 1283). |
| **1284** | John I becomes King of Jerusalem and Cyprus (until 1285). |
| **1285** | Henry II becomes king of Cyprus (nominal ruler until 1324); Mamluks take Margat. |
| **1287–89** | Crusade led by Alice of Blois reaches Acre; Mamluks take Latakia and Tripoli. |
| **1290** | Northern Italian Crusade to the Holy Land. |
| **1291** | Mamluks take Acre, Sidon and Beirut; Crusaders evacuate Tartus and Atlit. |
| **1299** | Mongols defeat a Mamluk army near Homs, leading to temporary revival of Crusading optimism in Europe. |
| **1302** | Mamluks retake Arwad island; probable end of Crusader rule at Jbayl. |

The seemingly isolated tower of Burj al-Sabi overlooks the coastal road south of Banyas. It was strong enough to impose tolls upon travellers but the main fortress in this area was Margat, which rises a short distance inland. This tower is also said to have been linked to Marqab by a long wall.

# The development of Crusader fortifications

The 13th century saw a number of significant changes in the design of European and Islamic fortifications, the most significant of which first appeared in the Middle East. Consequently, the development of military architecture within the Crusader States played an important role in the history of medieval castles. At the same time major differences remained between inland and coastal fortifications. The remaining inland sites tended to be compact and relatively inaccessible when compared with some sprawling coastal cities. However, the inland city of Antioch was an exception, and also differed from most large coastal cities in having a naturally defensible position. Most coastal towns and cities lay on relatively flat and exposed terrain. This was even true of Acre, which despite being located on a headland required massive fortifications along its landward sides. Being both the effective if not titular capital of the Kingdom of Jerusalem, and by far the most populous Crusader city, it demanded special attention.

The biggest design changes became apparent in the early 13th century, reflecting developments in urban and citadel construction in neighbouring Syria. However, Crusader military architects were already improving upon existing styles during the late 12th century (see Fortress 21: *Crusader Castles in the Holy Land 1097–1192*), adopting and adapting, copying from others and making improvements of their own. As yet their fortifications still relied on massive and sometimes isolated towers stemming from Western European traditions, plus the Romano-Islamic castrum fortified enclosure and the new double castrum concept, which largely dated from the 12th century. Crusader architects also used naturally defensible features when siting fortifications on hilltops, mountain spurs or coastal headlands. In fact these designers demonstrated considerable adaptability while responding to the nature of a site, the size, importance, function and proposed garrison of a building. The often limited amount of money available for construction is frequently overlooked by observers who criticise the roughness of some Crusader structures. Simple rectangular towers were still built during the 13th century, though, one example being Qal'at Jiddin.

In low-lying or open regions, castra still served as regional defences against raiding or small-scale invasions, though most dated from before the Battle of Hattin. The original Sea Castle at Sidon may be such a castrum. The gate of this unusual fort faced the land, with a broad outer and a narrower inner arch with a slit for a portcullis between. Above the outer arch was a large machicolation supported by four stone brackets. Beneath each outer bracket was a carved lion, with human figures on the inner brackets. A bridge to the gate was supported by massive rectangular piers with triangular eastern sides to break the force of the waves. Stone arches spanned the gaps, except for the innermost, which orginally had a wooden drawbridge raised by chains from the machicolation.

Most double castra, hilltop and spur castles were sited in border areas, serving as garrison bases or protected depots containing supplies for field armies. Nevertheless, some scholars have misunderstood their function, dismissing some mountain castles as 'not very impressive' and failing to appreciate the importance of location. In fact, most complex spur and hilltop Crusader fortifications date from the 13th century. This might reflect new military priorities, although most Crusader inland territory now consisted of mountainous or upland terrain.

The most detailed documentary source about the construction of a 13th-century fortification deals with a hilltop castle. The *De constructione castri*

Small fragments of wall paintings have been found in several 13th-century Crusader castles. Most are in a distinctive style, which combined western European, Byzantine and Syrian Christian elements. To gain a better idea of what these paintings once looked like, it is necessary to travel beyond the area conquered by the Crusaders, to the remarkable monastery of Mar Musa al-Habashi in the hills north-east of Damascus. The interior of the church is all but covered with paintings of mounted warrior saints and biblical scenes in the same mixed style. Here, for example, St. Bacchus uses a western European form of saddle, which is even painted with heraldic decorations.

*Saphet* discusses the Templar rebuilding of Safad after 1240. The huge costs came to 1.1 million 'Saracen bezants' for the first two and a half years, followed by 40,000 per year thereafter. A peacetime garrison was to include 50 brother knights, 30 brother sergeants, 50 turcopoles, 300 archers, 820 workmen and other staff, and 400 slaves; in wartime their number was expected to reach 2,200.

The fortified Monastery of St. Simeon the Younger, in the mountains west of Antioch, was presumably a much less expensive fortification. The best-preserved fragment is the western gateway in an outer wall, which formed one of three concentric barriers. Its crude construction made use of material from the inner wall. A third construction programme on a western gateway using well-cut ashlar blocks probably dates from the late Crusader period.

The majority of 13th-century Crusader spur-castles are in the northern and eastern regions, where the largest dominated passes or important roads. Several could accommodate large garrisons and one of the biggest problems faced by their designers was guaranteeing adequate water supplies. According to the Arab chronicler al-Dimashqi around 1300, Hisn Akkar (Gibelcar) had a 'channel of water coming right into the castle, brought down from the hills above, and sufficient both for domestic purposes and for drinking'. Its remains can still be seen. At Montfort the keep was built above a massive cistern. Water might have been a problem in some spur-castles, but their locations on steep promontories gave designers a clear topographical advantage. This was usually enhanced by cutting a fosse across the spur, separating the castle from the neighbouring hill.

## Powerful siege weaponry

However, the most dramatic and expensive change came in the early decades of the 13th century, and was a response to a large-scale adoption of powerful counterweight trebuchets. The principle of the counterweight stone-throwing machine had probably been known for considerably longer than is generally realised (see New Vanguard 69: *Medieval Siege Weapons (2) Byzantium, the Islamic World & India AD 476–1526*), but it was only from the late 12th century onwards that such weapons were used in large numbers. Furthermore, the counterweight trebuchet initially made its greatest impact in defence rather than attack, as a counter-battery weapon that was most effective when mounted on top of a tower.

This led to a sudden appearance of larger, broader, and deeper towers, serving as artillery emplacements. Some fortresses had one such 'great tower' placed on the most vulnerable side, sometimes as a further development of the main keep. Where a larger area was enclosed the result could be a series of massive towers linked by relatively traditional curtain walls. It was a true revolution in fortification, and it was not until the widespread adoption of siege cannon in the 15th century that anything as fundamental would be seen again.

Another important development was a multiplication of existing defensive features, including doubled walls, more numerous towers and an abundance of embrasures in the walls. Tiers of superimposed defensive galleries with loopholes were installed, along with various forms of projecting machicolation. While greater efforts were made to use naturally defensive features, walls also become thicker. Ancient columns were often laid horizontally through such walls, binding their inner and outer layers together, and there was increasing use of the Islamic talus, or sloping additional base, along the outer foot of a wall.

## Design influences

Despite the increasing sophistication of 13th-century Crusader fortifications, their designs still reflected the immediate circumstances; efforts to impose distinctive categories upon Templar or Hospitaller military architecture are misleading. Much more depended on local conditions, available local stone, and the origins, backgrounds and traditions of architects, masons and even labourers.

It has sometimes been suggested that the adoption of round towers in the early 13th century reflected Armenian influence, and the importance of non-western European military architecture has already been discussed in the preceding volume (Fortress 21: *Crusader Castles in the Holy Land 1097–1192*). Yet influences flowed in several directions and while there was Armenian influence on castles in the Principality of Antioch, there was comparable Crusader influence upon Armenian fortifications in neighbouring Cilicia. Elsewhere in the Kingdom of Cilician Armenia, the large castle of Silifke was largely built by or for the Hospitallers, who also rebuilt Tal Hamdun (Toprakkale), where a Mamluk castle later largely replaced the Hospitaller one. The Templars built a castle at Amoude, were largely responsible for a castle at Trapesac, and made minor alterations to the existing Islamic castle at Haruniya; all of which were at various times within the Armenian kingdom. However, these tended to be different from one another, again reflecting the primacy of local considerations.

ABOVE AND LEFT The outer wall of the small castle of Castel Rouge (al-Qal'at Yahmur) has only one corner tower (ABOVE). Its barrel-vaulted interior is rather cramped but is provided with arrow slits for crossbowmen (LEFT).

15

The castle of le Destroit (Khirbat Dustray), was constructed on the low coastal ridge of central Palestine to control the coastal road between Haifa and Jaffa. It played a major role during the Third Crusade. It stood on a rock-cut base and many of its internal structures were partially cut from the rock. The narrow coastal ridge was itself cut by a ditch, perhaps during the early 13th century; this served as a sort of dry moat on the southern side of the castle.

Islamic influence is more obvious, though the identity of those responsible for a specific structure can remain problematical. For example, the castle of Belfort overlooking the western side of the Litani gorge in southern Lebanon began as a simple 12th-century tower-keep, approximately 12m square. Later additions included a vaulted hall and a broad enclosed area with rounded towers. A rock-cut fosse contained cisterns and during the 13th century further outworks strengthened the southern side of Belfort. This resulted in a barbican in the upper ward dominating the lower ward. A new chapel was added and eventually both wards were almost filled with vaulted structures. However, archaeological work has shown that by the time the Crusaders finally lost the castle of Belfort, it already included a hexagonal tower added by the Ayyubids during their previous domination of the site. Much of the outer works and the entrance ramp are now lost. However, relics of a vast strengthening programme carried out by the Mamluks during the second half of the 13th century remain.

There were as yet no European parallels for the cramped, box-type machicolations seen at Crac des Chevaliers, though these did exist in the Islamic citadels of Aleppo, Damascus and elsewhere. In fact the similarities are so striking that the same stonemasons might have been employed by both Muslims and Christians. Some doubts have been raised about the windmill on a tower at Crac des Chevaliers, though the evidence is strong. Windmills originated in Iran and spread to Europe during the Middle Ages, so perhaps Crusader castles like Crac des Chevaliers played a part in this process of technological transfer.

## Urban defences: Ascalon and Acre

With regard to urban fortifications, efforts were initially focused upon citadels rather than the walls around a town. Most such work was done during the decades of relative peace, when Egypt and Syria were ruled by the Ayyubids. Examples include the Castle of Richard of Cornwall, built in 1241 in the north-western corner of Ascalon, which the Crusaders briefly regained. Here a new concentric citadel had a rock-cut ditch to the south and east. To the north was the city wall of Ascalon, here fronted by a masonry talus, and some marble slabs crudely carved with the arms of Sir Hugh Wake of Lincolnshire date from this period. A few years later the French King Louis IX built a second castle at Sidon, known as the Land Castle to distinguish it from Sidon's more famous Sea Castle. It was built upon the massive remains of a Romano-Byzantine theatre and used the ancient stone seats as building blocks.

From Louis IX's Crusade onwards, greater efforts were put into fortifying the urban areas. Previously citizens had been vulnerable to enemy raiding, sometimes even being plundered by local bedouin. It was assumed that such raiders merely wanted portable loot, and would leave once satisfied. Meanwhile the town's inhabitants took refuge in a citadel with their most valuable property, then returned to their homes in the largely unprotected outer city once the raiders departed. The rise of the Mamluk Sultanate changed this, and the determined campaigns of reconquest launched by Mamluk armies resulted

Although the tall Crusader castle, or citadel, on the northern side of the town of Arsuf has almost entirely collapsed, the lower parts of its wall still include very interesting details. For example, the main gate seen here included two carved stone sills or 'curbs' across the road; a deep groove that was probably for a sliding portcullis; and the metallic anchor point for the bottom of a heavy wooden door, visible as a small dark rectangle in the floor next to the wall.

in more efforts to surround the remaining Crusader towns with proper fortifications including some massive gates. The towers spaced along curtain walls were usually rectangular, though there was one rounded tower at Atlit, while Ascalon had both rounded and triangular ones.

The partially demolished defences of Ascalon were already so strong that late 12th- and 13th-century Crusader work largely consisted of repairs and embellishments. Here the construction included outworks with occasional casemates, four towers with indirect access and at least 14 other towers of rectangular, half-round or triangular plan; some strengthened with reused, horizontally laid, ancient or early medieval columns. The town's four gates similarly incorporated reused Roman and early Islamic elements. In addition to his new Land Castle at Sidon, Louis IX built massive walls around the town itself, with a deep moat and an entrance known as the Tyre Gate between two strong towers. Most of this has been lost, but Louis' walls around Caesarea Maritima on the Palestinian coast largely survive. They have been excavated by Israeli archaeologists and now stand as the finest existing examples of 13th-century Crusader urban fortification.

Until the Third Crusade, Acre had only a single wall but in its aftermath the city and its expanding northern suburb of Montmussard were given doubled walls, numerous massive towers and a deep ditch or moat. These were further strengthened by King Louis IX. Sadly almost all have now disappeared and even their position remains a matter of debate. Recent archaeological excavation and new analysis of the documentary sources are clarifying the issue. The northern walls were probably further north than believed and Acre, plus Montmussard, were much larger than had been realised.

Some of the most useful evidence comes from aerial photography before what is now called the Old City of Acre expanded. These include reconnaissance photographs taken by the Ottoman Turkish Air Force during the First World War, which clearly show the foundations of a wall that looks like the northern defences of Acre-Montmussard. They also show the coastal marsh, now drained, which lay just beyond that wall. A short section of wall uncovered in 1935 lay on this line, while a remarkable number of stone mangonel balls were found on a small promontory where it reached the sea – almost certainly dating from the 1291 siege.

Within the Old City were several large fortified structures, plus the *torre* (tall fortified towers) of the Italian merchant communes. They included the Castle of the King's Constable and the massive Convent or Headquarters of the

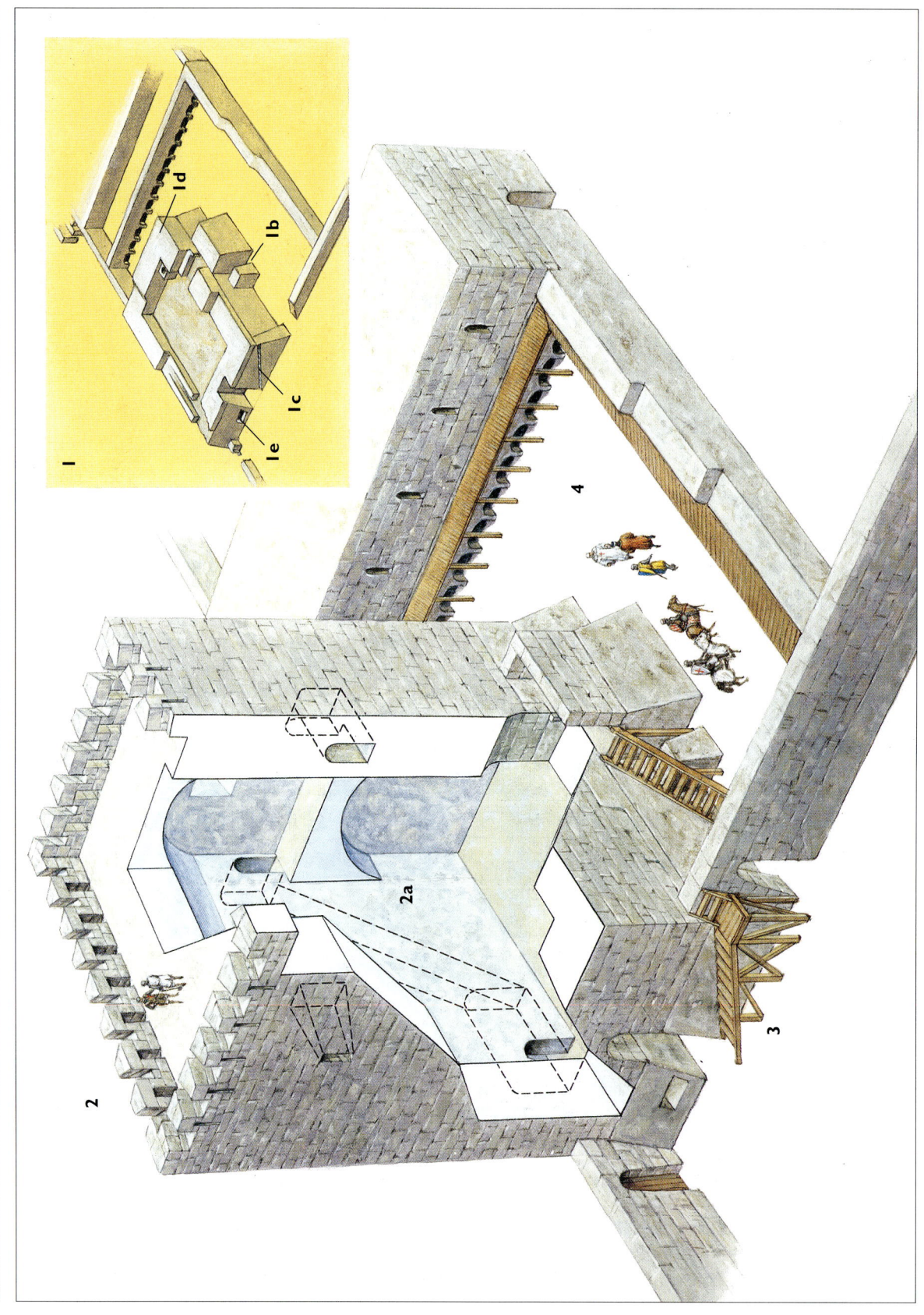

1

1d

1b

1c

1e

4

2

2a

3

18

The lower chambers of Crusader castles were almost invariably much plainer than the sometimes decorated and better illuminated upper chambers. Those seen here are in Crac des Chevaliers, and are sometimes described as barracks. However, they are more likely to have been used as storerooms for food for the garrison and its horses, or for munitions.

Hospitallers, both adjacent to the 12th-century city wall separating Acre proper from Montmussard. Close to the main harbour stood the Court of the Chain and the Venetian 'market', both massive enough to be fortifications in their own right. The Templar Burgus or Castle stood on the shore at the south-western corner of the city. Early aerial photography and recent archaeological investigations indicate that the eastern wall lay further east than once thought. As a result it now seems that later 13th-century Acre enclosed an area considerably larger than pre-Crusader Islamic Acre, whose layout had been established in the 9th century.

The most significant recent excavation concerning the fortifications of Crusader Acre took place in what is called the Courtyard site, outside what had been regarded as the 13th-century city. Here a team of Israeli archaeologists uncovered a postern gate and a tower, both probably built between 1198 and 1212. A wide pilaster in a corner of the tower may have supported wooden stairs to the upper floors. A plaster-lined water basin was constructed inside one corner of the tower and the designers even inserted a well shaft within the core of the circuit wall, suggesting that the tower served as a service area as well as a fortification. Furthermore, the archaeologists discovered fragments of Crusader pottery, including a cooking pot, an amphora, a drinking jug, some bowls containing chicken bones and two decorated glass vessels plus evidence of a cooking fire. Perhaps the tower was a kitchen? Its walls were vertical with no glacis, and beyond them a moat was cut through earlier Hellenistic and Byzantine remains. The plastered upper floor of the tower had not been carried on stone vaults, as was usual, but on wooden joists, and the upper chamber itself was probably used as soldiers' living quarters.

### The fortified way-station of Le Destroit in the late 12th century

Le Destroit was built on a system of foundations excavated from the rock. It commanded a defile through a low ridge parallel to the shore, along which the north–south road ran until modern times. These fortifications played a vital role during the Third Crusade, but in 1220 Le Destroit was demolished by the Templars and was replaced by the stronger fortress of Atlit. Today only the rock-cut foundations (1) and some of the lower course of masonry remains. The tower (2) originally consisted of a vaulted chamber with a staircase within its north wall (2a) leading to an upper chamber; this hypothetical reconstruction is based upon similar towers within the Kingdom of Jerusalem. The stone-cut foundation plinth contained cisterns on its eastern (1d) and western (1e) sides, plus rock-cut supports for an entrance stair on the south (1b). Peg-holes on the western slope (1c) may have been for a wooden stair to a wall between two main yards (3). The inner yard (4) contained rows of rock-cut mangers, once covered by simple wooden roofs. Whether any of the outer rock-cut areas were roofed is unknown. (After Dikijian and Nicolle)

ABOVE LEFT The Hospitaller Convent or headquarters in Acre, sometimes called the Citadel, was built on and around earlier structures. These included some Fatimid fortifications, probably dating from the 11th century. Here the Islamic walls can still be seen inside the larger western wall of the Hospitaller fortification.

ABOVE RIGHT The French King Louis VII offered to pay for the construction of the refectory in the Hospitallers' main Convent or headquarters in Acre. This may account for the presence of at least two carved fleurs-de-lis, the French royal coat-of-arms, in the otherwise undecorated Convent hall.

These remains formed part of the outer wall of 13th-century Acre but were well beyond the line of the inner wall, as excavated in the mid 1980s. The tower itself is likely to have been one of those between the doubled wall around Montmussard and the north-eastern corner of the city proper. According to written sources, there were three towers here: the Venetian Tower, the English Tower and the King's Tower. Of these the King's Tower was the most important, marking the north-eastern corner itself. However, it was round, whereas the tower at the Courtyard site was square. Though it was destroyed by fire, there is no evidence of a major attack upon this structure, and because it seems to be so close to Montmussard it should probably be identified as the Venetian rather than the English Tower.

## Construction methods and 'engigneors'

The methods of construction seen in 13th-century Crusader castles differed little from those of the previous century. Meanwhile, documentary sources shed an interesting light on the men who actually designed or supervised the construction of Crusader fortifications – the *engigneors*. These men were not merely military engineers but were often multi-talented individuals with numerous different skills. They could have high status, though not being members of the aristocratic elite, and appear to have been recruited from various ethnic groups including Greeks, Armenians and Jews and Western Europeans.

Other specialists included men whose task was to feed and clothe the people on the building site. In addition to those involved in building work, soldiers defended the place and the resulting numbers could run into the tens of thousands. Perhaps because some projects were now so huge, these numbers had increased during the early 13th century, resulting in the effective conscription of some local populations who were then organised into what was almost an army of militarised artisan-soldiers. Prisoners of war could also be used as slave labour, but they required close supervision and were not entrusted with responsible tasks.

Details of construction techniques inevitably differed according to the nature of the terrain, and archaeological excavations show some unusual variations. For example, when the Crusaders refortified Ascalon they built thick walls with narrow courses of dressed ashlar around a poured concrete core with through columns. These were raised on a sloping artificial mound, largely of sand, and rising to a height of up to 10m with horizontal offsets at approximately one- to two-metre intervals. The mound was then lined with stone to form a glacis.

At Arsuf, the town's circuit wall was again built on sand foundations. The reasons are not entirely clear, but may have helped the structure absorb earthquakes, which are common in this region, and allowed water to drain beneath the walls. This was an architectural idea which long pre-dated the arrival of the Crusaders, yet it caused problems for modern archaeologists. For example, while the sand foundations at Arsuf were being studied, a family of foxes decided that they were an ideal place to excavate a home, causing the medieval wall to crack. Efforts to drive away the foxes failed, until the placing of lion's faeces from a helpful zoo finally convinced the foxes that they were no longer 'top predators', whereupon they moved elsewhere. Whether the engineers of medieval Arsuf and Ascalon faced similar problems is not recorded.

Given the variety of very localised problems, one would expect Crusader castle builders to have employed local masons with local experience. Yet the Military Orders that built castles in Cilicia rarely relied on Armenian masons. On the other hand the Crusaders used ancient or early medieval building material where this was available. When constructing the Sea Castle at Sidon they apparently hauled such masonry from the shallow sea.

So many variations were involved in these buildings that it is difficult to distinguish Crusader and Islamic work. However, one idea that does seem to have spread from east to west was the use of embossed masonry. This had been known in the Middle East since ancient times but did not appear in western Europe – with the possible exception of Alsace – before the 13th century. It offered additional protection against missiles, since the bosses ensured that mangonel balls rarely struck a wall square but normally hit a glancing blow. Their appearance at Acre and Tyre at the start of the 13th century might be further evidence for the increasing importance of large trebuchets in siege warfare.

Another distinctive feature in the Sea Castle at Sidon was the use of some dry-stone construction, presumably because the available mortar would not set properly when in contact with seawater. There were continued references to iron cramps or pins being used to strengthen Crusader fortifications, sometimes set into lead, though the iron at Sidon seems to have been driven

This carved marble slab was found in the ruins of Ascalon. It consists of a fine Arabic inscription made during the pre-Crusader Fatimid period, to which the repeated coat-of-arms of Sir Hugh Wake of Lincolnshire were crudely added in the mid 13th century.

The Tower of Flies once guarded the entrance to the outer harbour of Acre. A mole may originally have enclosed the southern side of this harbour, extending from the base of the tower to the seaward end of the inner eastern wall of the city.

into wood. More wood was, in fact, used in the construction of Crusader castles than is generally realised. Many roofs were of timber, especially for outbuildings such as stables. Large amounts of timber were similarly used for scaffolding.

The well-known manuscript called *De constructione castri Saphet* was made for Armand du Périgord, Grand Master of the Templars, and is dated 1264. It provides details about the Crusaders' attempts to refortify Safad in the 1240s, but was previously regarded as controversial because it apparently did not fit the evidence of the site. For example it mentioned an internal rampart (*in muris*), and a foss (*fossatis*) within an external wall (*antemuralia*) which itself had a moat (*scama*) and seven towers. Also the garrison appeared impossibly numerous. In fact the Mamluks besieged Safad in 1266 and when the castle capitulated the victors reportedly found a garrison of 4,000 soldiers. However, more recent archaeological work shows that the document of 1264 was much closer to reality than expected.

Even more detailed information about 13th-century construction techniques was uncovered at the so-called Courthouse site in Acre, which exposed part of the Crusader city's outer wall, a tower and part of the moat with a masonry counterscarp. The tower was made of ashlar, pieces of which featured traces of plaster, suggesting they had previously been used elsewhere. The outer ashlar was finely finished and was laid in mortar 3cm thick. But the ashlar stones of the inner face were not so well dressed, with smaller stones being added to level the courses or fill gaps. This inner face was then plastered. The core of the wall was almost 2m thick, consisting of concrete into which rough 'field' stones and dressed stones were irregularly set. Evidence from other Crusader sites indicates that such inner cores were not just dumped inside the outer facings. In many cases they were carefully made and proved just as strong as the regular facings. The city wall of Acre, as exposed at the Courthouse site, was about 3m thick at its base, tapering slightly as it rose. It was laid upon bedrock, which is today not only below the water table but below the current sea level. However, the sea level has changed since the 13th century. The lower three courses were of large dressed stones, and a vertical seam, which does not continue in the higher courses, shows that the planners decided to enlarge the tower after work had already begun. The bottom of the moat corresponded to the third course of stones, and above these foundations the upper part of the wall was built of smooth ashlar.

# The principles of defence

The 13th century was not only a period of revolutionary change in the design of Crusader fortifications, but also in strategic priorities. The main efforts were now focused upon the protection of people rather than territory and in some places the numbers to be defended were very high. Acre was the biggest city, but Crusader-ruled Antioch still had a population of around 100,000 people, mostly Greeks and other non-Catholic Christians. Another feature of this period was the growth of suburbs next to major fortresses, mostly defended by a single wall. Crusader-held territory now consisted of parts of the eastern Mediterranean coast with the sea to the west and hills or mountains to the east. This strip had, in fact, been cut in two by Saladin's reconquest of some of the coast north of Latakia. Some castles were sited to cover the few east–west routes through which Islamic armies might enter Crusader territory, but it was just as important to locate fortifications on the coast, to hinder movement by invaders who reached it. Furthermore, the Crusader States were now entirely dependent upon contact with, and support from, Europe. The protection of ports and harbours was thus essential. By the 13th century, European fleets dominated the Mediterranean, and without them the Crusader States could not have survived as long as they did. Nevertheless, this domination was not complete and the Mamluks made several efforts to revive the Egyptian navy. Meanwhile, smaller Turkish fleets based along what are now the Mediterreanean and Aegean coasts of Turkey grew increasingly daring.

The perennial problem of ensuring reliable supplies of drinking water resulted in extraordinary care being taken in the fortified Hospitaller headquarters in Acre, with every drop of rain from the wet season being stored. This was not only for drinking but also for hygiene, such as the flushing of the communal toilets; two parallel water systems being kept scrupulously separate. However, Islamic architects always demonstrated a little more sophistication in such matters, and in many fortifications the most impressive water storage cisterns date from Mamluk rebuilding rather than from the Crusader period. One example is in the castle at Safad where a circular large cistern, excavated from rock then covered by a masonry dome, lay beneath the great Mamluk tower at the southern part of the site.

The Crusader States' shortage of military manpower was also growing more acute. Architectural and engineering skills could help greatly, but could not solve this problem definitively; as a result, most 13th-century Crusader fortifications were designed for small garrisons. Large garrisons existed, though rarely, and they were usually mustered for offensive purposes. In fact many Crusader castles were gravely undermanned when the final crisis came. Belfort is said to have had 22 knights and 400 other men when it was besieged by a Mamluk army in 1268. Even so the Mamluk Sultan Baybars still felt the need to bring 28 powerful siege machines against it.

Whether a reliance on fortification made the Crusader States vulnerable to the Mamluks' highly developed forms of psychological warfare seems doubtful. This interpretation of events probably reflects the attitudes of 19th- and 20th-century military historians rather than the realities of 13th-century Middle Eastern warfare. Another myth concerns a supposed system of visible communication between Crusader castles. According to this theory, those in Cilicia formed part of an elaborate network. However, most were not in actual or useful line-of-sight with each other and the Crusader States' hypothetical chain of signal beacons probably never existed. The good visibility enjoyed by such garrisons stemmed from the fact that they were stationed on hilltops for defensive reasons, not for communication.

Height was always sought after, although the emphasis on defending the weakest slope meant that the strongest part of a fortification was not necessarily at its highest point. On the other hand, locating a castle on a high place often limited its internal space. Haruniya, for example, was given to the Teutonic Knights in 1236. Here a largely 10th-century Islamic fort was in the hands of a Latin lord by the late 12th century. It consisted of a cramped central courtyard within a shell keep with two floors of shooting galleries and a rounded tower. The Teutonic Knights probably repaired the tower and perhaps used it as a chapel, but did little else. The northern Lebanese castle of Gibelcar was similarly cramped and rudimentary. Yet the site is so inaccessible that Sultan Baybars found it as difficult to take as the far larger and more sophisticated castle at Crac des Chevaliers. In the event Baybars' sense of achievement when Gibelcar finally fell is reflected in a letter he wrote to Prince Bohemond VI of Antioch:

'We have transported the mangonels there through mountains where the birds think it too difficult to nest; how patiently we have hauled them, troubled by mud and struggling against rain.'

The citadels that defended a town or served as places of refuge for the inhabitants faced different problems. They were almost always easier to access than mountaintop or spur castles and could be vulnerable to attack from within the town if it fell to an enemy. In fact urban areas often provided good positions for mangonels to hurl stones against a citadel. A different problem was caused if a suburb extended around or beyond the citadel, leaving the latter as a fortified enclave within the urban area. This happened at Acre, where the Castle of the King's Constable and the Convent of the Hospitallers lost much of their original value following the fortification of Montmussard.

Crusader urban defences usually had an outer ditch, often with a counterscarp wall. In many places all or part of the city wall was revetted with a sloping talus. Outer walls and barbicans were not universal in the Crusader States and do not seem to have been used in western Europe before the 13th century. In most places the walls themselves consisted of the previous Islamic defences, more or less improved, as was the case at Arsuf, though here the existing city walls were considerably strengthened. The main changes were usually the addition of larger towers along the curtain wall, and occasionally the building of a second wall. At Acre the resulting defences were particularly impressive. So much so that during the final siege of 1291, the Mamluk army needed a massive and prolonged bombardment using a very large number of the most powerful trebuchets before they could break into the city.

These new-style towers were much more formidable than those built in the 12th century, clearly impressing pilgrims like Wilbrand von Oldenburg, who visited Acre in 1212:

'This is a fine and strong city situated on the seashore in such a way that, while it is quadrangular in shape, two of its sides forming an angle are girdled and protected by the sea. The other two are encompassed by a fine, wide and deep ditch, stone lined to the very bottom, and by a double wall fortified with towers according to a fine arrangement, in such a way that the first wall with its towers does not overtop the main (second) wall and is commanded and defended by the second and inner wall, the towers of which are tall and very strong.'

This meant that arrows shot from the inner wall could be aimed over the outer wall, which was about one-third lower than the inner. The towers were also staggered so that those in front did not obstruct archers in the rear towers.

The great castle of Crac des Chevaliers was similarly ringed by an outer wall, which is generally believed to date from the early 13th century. The normal interpretation of Crac des Chevalier's fortification maintains that the inner defences were strengthened after this outer wall was added, while the southern side of the castle was given massive new-style towers around this time, almost certainly serving as artillery emplacements.

The defences of Atlit castle were similarly designed with defensive artillery in mind. Here three rectangular gate towers were placed approximately 44m apart. They had two floors and were surmounted by a platform enclosed by a parapet. All three projected about 12m from the curtain wall. Behind them was an inner wall with two huge towers approximately 28m long by 18m deep, both of which were originally over 34m high. Their great size and height reflected their role as artillery bastions to bombard enemy artillery, or at least keep it at a reasonable distance.

The greatly increased number of archery embrasures, niches, machicolations and other wall features indicated that crossbows played a very significant role in the defence of 13th-century Crusader fortifications. Some sources refer to 'underground vaults' where 'great-crossbows' could be sited; these being found in Louis IX's city walls of Caesarea, probably in the citadel of Arsuf, and perhaps forming a continuous line of niched embrasures in curtain walls and towers. It is also interesting to note the similarity in some details of design and construction, which almost suggest a conscious programme of refortification in the mid-13th-century Kingdom of Jerusalem.

The top of a rock-cut cistern next to the fortified manor house at Khirbat Rushmiyah, on Mount Carmel above Haifa. The carefully carved edge of the opening shows that it was designed to have a lid, perhaps of wood or stone. The chamber inside expands into a large bottle shape.

Comparable details are found in Crac des Chevaliers, where the outer wall and towers had archery slits to minimise the area of dead ground. These were staggered to avoid weakening the wall and to enable archers to command the area in front of the walls. Similarly a stone-vaulted chemin-de-ronde gave access to box machicolations. However, the cramped interiors of these machicolations meant that crossbowmen squatted or knelt to shoot. The entrance to Crac des Chevaliers was greatly strengthened, resulting in a highly developed bent entrance system, the whole length of which had 'murder holes' overlooking it. Although Crac des Chevaliers was a large castle, the space between its inner and outer walls remained so narrow that it could not be used as an outer bailey. The vulnerable south-eastern side of this gap consisted of an open water tank fed by an aqueduct from the neighbouring hill, both as a water supply and perhaps to inhibit mining. The massive inner walls followed those of the 12th-century castle but were built slightly outside the earlier fortification, leaving a narrow passage that was developed as a shooting gallery on the western and southern sides.

However, the southern and western walls were the most impressive, rising from a sloping glacis from which huge round towers emerged. There was even a shooting chamber within some parts of this glacis. Unfortunately, most of the wall-head defences have gone, though traces along the southern wall showed no machicolations. Instead there were arrow slits and larger rectangular openings, perhaps for great-crossbows or espringals.

The design of the walls of Acre meant that any part of the curtain wall that was breached was still covered by crossbowmen in the neighbouring towers.

The original name of the Crusader manor house at Khirbat Rushmiyah is uncertain. The complex consists of a tower whose basement is partly groin vaulted and partly barrel vaulted. A rectangular forebuilding was added later, perhaps in the 13th century, and may have contained a staircase. Meanwhile the main door was protected by arrow slits.

### The entrance complex of Crac des Chevaliers, mid 13th century

Some of the smaller or less important Crusader castles had small resident garrisons, and in some cases no permanent garrisons at all. However, major fortified locations like Crac des Chevaliers housed a considerable number of people and animals, and this number could reach a remarkable level in times of crisis. Consequently even Crac des Chevaliers could get crowded. Small postern gates in the outer walls of such castles were not normally used for entry and exit,

so at Crac des Chevaliers everything had to use the main east gate. Behind this was a long, covered, dog-leg entrance ramp (shown here) leading to the centre of the castle. It also went past what are believed to have been the main stables. Here, two war-horses are being brought out of the inner stables by their grooms; having been inside the stables for some time, one of the horses has reared up, as its owner watches, to the right. Behind the horse, a column of baggage donkeys coming down the exit ramp with their handlers has been held up by the commotion.

The entrance complex of Crac des Chevaliers, mid 13th century

Considerable emphasis was also placed on the fortification of gates; so much so that these were rarely attacked. They could include a drawbridge, portcullis and panels in the doors, plus embrasures to increase the number of shooting positions within the gateway. Limitations of space may have been why bent-gates were not always employed. At Atlit the three gate towers had straight-through entrances, two with a portcullis and one possibly having a slit machicolation. In contrast, two of the three gates at Caesarea were certainly bent. Each had a slit machicolation and a portcullis protecting the doors while the inner doors were defended by a slit machicolation. Most town gates, however strongly fortified, were less complicated than those of castles or citadels. The latter tended to have adjacent towers while access to the interior was usually via one or more right-angle bends, often through gate chambers that could be sealed off by the defenders.

Postern gates allowed sorties by the defenders if any attackers came too close. One of the last Hospitaller constructions at Crac des Chevaliers was a postern, built between 1254 and 1269. It had a tower on each side plus a portcullis and probably machicolations. The small castle of Cursat may have included an unusual postern, which seems to have been associated with a cistern, several underground apartments and a vertical shaft cut into the rock. This led from a subterranean complex in the eastern part of the castle, down to a lower chamber at the level of the base of the ramparts. The associated masonry probably dates from the late 12th or early 13th century and the vertical shaft may have been excavated after an upper firing platform was already in place. Perhaps archers climbed down the shaft to cover a small postern gate. Elsewhere some posterns opened several metres above the base of the wall, and were only reached by ropes or a ladder.

This complex at Cursat apparently made use of an existing crack in the rock that was subsequently enlarged; Crusader military architects often made use of available natural features. On the coast these included the sea itself. At Atlit a small promontory was cut by a moat, and although the available technology did not permit the excavation of deep sea-filled moats, the rock could be cut away to just below sea level. Since then, however, part of the coast has sunk, leaving some 'sea moats' deeper than they were in the Middle Ages.

The few safe harbours along the Crusader-held coast were vital for the survival of the Crusader States, and so were given special attention. Most consisted of small bays, sometimes sheltered by reefs or rocks. Man-made harbours (moles) existed at Acre, Arsuf, Atlit, Caesarea, Beirut, Sidon and Tyre in the Kingdom of Jerusalem, while others served the County of Tripoli and the Principality of Antioch.

In several places towers stood at the ends of such moles; one such being the Tower of Flies at Acre. This was garrisoned by guards, who checked the identities of ships, the arrival of which was indicated by the tolling of a bell, perhaps in this tower. Towers could also be armed with anti-shipping siege machines, which threatened to sink vessels that attacked the boom. Other towers served as anchor points for chains or booms to close a harbour entrance, like the floating wooden 'chain' constructed across Acre harbour by the Genoese during their quarrel with the Venetians in 1258.

Harbours were themselves usually separated from a town by a wall. However, quays were rare and small boats usually carried goods between the beach and ships moored in the harbour. Elsewhere, Jaffa had a very exposed port, which had been refortified by the early Crusaders. It was strengthened during the following century, but still fell to the Mamluks in 1268. The Citadel of Arsuf is sometimes said to tower above a small harbour enclosed by two moles and a breakwater. However, the area in question may actually have been just above water during the Crusader occupation. So perhaps the moles and breakwater enclosed a flat area of flimsy buildings serving as a sort of foreshore beneath the castle and city.

# A tour of five Crusader fortifications

## Margat

William of Oldenburg described Margat as follows:

> A huge and very strong castle, defended by a double wall and protected by several towers. It stands on a high mountain … Every night four Knights of the Hospital and 28 soldiers keep guard there … The provisions stored there are sufficient for five years.

Margat's hilltop location is linked by a neck of land to a larger hill to the south, this potentially vulnerable approach being defended by a rock-cut reservoir to discourage mining. Margat itself is divided into two areas consisting of the castle and the fortified town, divided by a ditch and wall. The outer walls were defended by a dozen towers, of which all but four are round and probably date from after the Hospitallers had taken control.

Margat's defences are remarkably varied. On the eastern front, a wall and several round towers create a huge hillside terrace, behind which is a glacis crowned by an inner wall. How far this inner wall originally extended is, however, unclear. The north of the site has a single wall dominated by a square tower, probably from the 12th century. On the western side was an enclosure strengthened by four early 13th-century round towers whose wall-head defences are now lost. The main castle dominated the southern end of the enclosure, and was approached through a square gatehouse in the outer wall. Above the entrance arch are the corbels, which supported a machicolation; there is also a groove for a portcullis. The resulting complex entrance has alternative angled routes into the castle, though there was no access to the upper floors from the gate. Another fortified gate linked the fortress and the town, while the exterior of the citadel was protected by a double wall. On its western side are three square towers, again probably dating from the 12th century. The wall connecting them has a covered 'shooting gallery'. But on the other side there are no towers because the slope is so steep that simple walls

The great Hospitaller fortress of Margat crowns a steep hill overlooking the Mediterranean, near Banyas. The site consisted of a fortified town, on the right, and a much better protected citadel on the left. The southernmost outer bastion of this citadel was rebuilt by the Mamluks after they captured the place, and is distinguished by a horizontal line of white limestone masonry. Most of the rest of the fortress dates from the 12th and 13th century Crusader period.

Though plain and undecorated, the church inside the citadel of Margat is an impressive structure built of finely cut white limestone, in stark contrast to the roughly cut black basalt of the rest of the castle.

were considered adequate. At the very southern tip of this roughly triangular citadel was what the Crusaders called the Tower of the Spur, which was replaced by the great Mamluk tower that dominates the southern end of Margat.

These outer defences are overlooked by cliff-like inner walls, which surround the inner court; the latter is largely surrounded by vaulted halls used for storage and shelter. On the southern side is a more elegant, vaulted chamber, which was probably the Knights' Hall. Nearby is a grand but austere chapel whose eastern end was incorporated into the castle wall. It was probably built shortly after the Hospitallers gained possession of Margat, although the halls on each side are from a later period.

Numerous changes were made to the plan during the construction of Margat, and it seems almost as if the masons were working continuously, year after year. The result is ingenious if rather confusing, with the most impressive elements of the citadel being two massive round towers. The smaller of these, at the north-eastern corner, still has its wall-head defences, which consist, at the lower level, of arrow-slits and one large rectangular opening for a counter-siege machine. Above them a wall walk has merlons pierced with arrow slits. At the southern end, where the natural defences are weakest, the Hospitallers constructed a round keep, 200m in diameter and 24m high. It was comparable to the great circular keeps of western Europe, though somewhat squatter, perhaps because of the threat of earthquakes.

Otherwise the castle of Margat is remarkable for its use of superimposed halls and vaults, provided with arrow slits to turn them into huge shooting galleries, linked by a maze of often unlit staircases within the wall. Most

Today the western side of the fortress-town of Margat looks less impressive than the eastern and southern defences. This was, however, the original approach and was protected by two strong enclosure walls plus a dry moat. Most of what is visible here forms the inner wall with the mass of the main citadel rising on the right.

The inner courtyard of the great castle of Crac des Chevaliers is remarkably small because so much of its area has been covered by additional structures. Of these the most famous is the fine, carved, Gothic arcade on the right, which formed a covered cloister for the brothers of the Hospitaller Military Order.

probably served as storerooms or barracks though one contained ovens and some seem to have been stables. Above them is an extensive roof terrace, perhaps intended for stone-throwing siege machines of the type which defended Margat in 1285. In fact, numerous arrowheads embedded in the mortar around certain arrow slits probably date from the final siege.

The eastern entrance of the castle of Crac des Chevaliers led to a covered entrance ramp, the upper part of which is seen here. Halfway up the covered corridor the ramp made an abrupt 180-degree turn, at the furthest point visible in this picture.

## Crac des Chevaliers

Crac des Chevaliers, with its finely cut white limestone masonry, is less forbidding than the dark and roughly cut basalt mass of Margat. It is, however, more cramped, with approximately three-quarters of the area within the inner walls being built over. A chapel stands at one end of a small courtyard while at the other a large raised platform rests on vaults, which were probably used for storage, inner stabling and as shelter from incoming stones and arrows. On the western side of this courtyard is the magnificent Hall of the Knights, perhaps largely 12th century with 13th-century interior vaulting and ribs. However, even this was not the most remarkable aspect of Crac des Chevaliers. To quote the historian Hugh Kennedy:

The most striking feature is the gallery on the courtyard side, which probably dates from the 1230s; elegant, with delicate, slender pillars and tracery, it shows all the refinement of the high Gothic of the thirteenth century and is a perfect complement to the massive fortifications. There is a short Latin verse inscribed on one of the arches: *Sit tibi copia, Sit sapiencia, Formaque detur, Inquinat omnia sola, Superbia si comitetur.* (Have richness, have wisdom, have beauty but beware of pride, which spoils all it comes into contact with.)

In stern contrast to the delicacy of this carved gallery or cloister, are the great towers of the southern wall. These provided accommodation for the 60 or so knights who were the aristocracy of the community. The south-west tower also has a vaulted circular chamber, which may later have been modified to provide the Grand Master with some privacy. On top are the remains of a small watchtower.

## Atlit

The dramatic coastal castle of Atlit is now a closed military zone, and it remains to be seen how much damage is being caused by its use as a training area for Israeli marine commandos. However, it was well recorded during the British Mandate of the 1930s.

Otherwise known as Pilgrims' Castle, Atlit stands on a low promontory and was built from 1217 onwards. A fortified town was added later. The concentric defences of the castle itself are separated from the mainland by a rock-cut ditch and counterscarp wall in front of two massive walls. The inner wall is 12m thick and was over 30m high, being flanked by two rectangular towers. The outer is over 6m thick and was 15m high with three towers.

Beyond the castle, the town wall had a ditch and counterscarp, three gatehouses, each with a portcullis and probably slot machicolations. There were wooden bridges over the ditch, and an additional postern. A small harbour south of the castle provided limited protection from storms, and on the far side of the town was a stone-faced earthen rampart, which marked the southern edge of the precious salt-pans that brought considerable revenue to Atlit. The seaward end of this rampart also had a moated tower.

One of the most remarkable features inside the castle of Crac des Chevaliers is an open cistern, or short moat, between the extremely strong southern outer wall, on the left, and the even larger southern glacis of the inner citadel, on the right. In addition to serving as a secure source of water, its existence may have inhibited mining operations against the vulnerable southern side of the castle.

The Templar castle of Atlit, or Pilgrims' Castle, seen from the ruins of the 12th-century castle of Le Destroit, which it replaced. Atlit castle was in a very strong position, which could be directly resupplied and supported from the sea. Consequently it resisted long after the now abandoned town of Atlit (to the left of this picture) had fallen to the Mamluks. The Templars also gained considerable revenue from valuable salt-evaporation pans seen in the foreground.

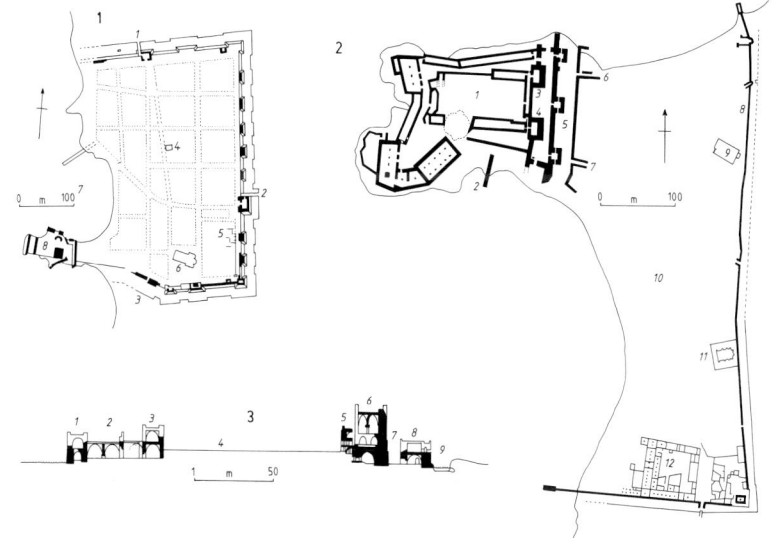

(1) Caesarea Maritima: 1 – North Gate; 2 – East Gate; 3 – Sea Gate; 4 – excavated Crusader building; 5 – excavated Crusader houses; 6 – Cathedral of St. Peter; 7 – port; 8 – Citadel. (After Benvenisti and Kaufmann)

(2) Atlit: 1 – inner ward of the Citadel; 2 – harbour; 3 – North Great Tower; 4 – South Great Tower; 5 – outer wall; 6 – north Beach Gate; 7 – south Beach Gate; 8 – urban fortified wall; 9 – baths; 10 – faubourg, or town; 11 – unfinished church; 12 – stables. (After Johns and Pringle)

(3) Section through the Citadel of Atlit (surviving structures are shown in black): 1 – north-west tower; 2 – north-west hall; 3 – west undercroft; 4 – inner ward; 5 – east quarters; 6 – north gate tower; 7 – east bailey; 8 – outer wall; 9 – fosse. (After Pringle)

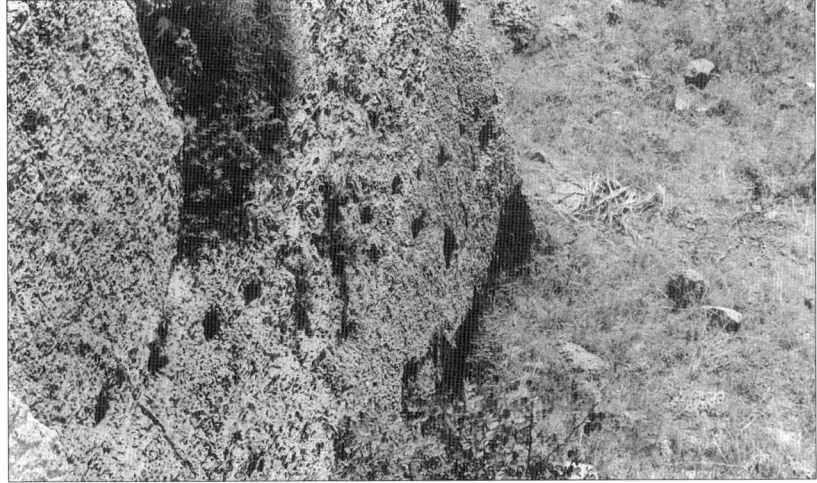

LEFT ABOVE The main entrance into Le Destroit, on the low coastal ridge next to Atlit castle, was a gateway partially cut through the rock. Another secondary entrance seems to have been approached via an external wooden stair supported on timber beams, which were slotted into a series of holes in the man-made rock face, as seen here.

LEFT BELOW Atlit in the 1930s, looking inland from the castle across the valuable salt-pans to the coastal plain and hills of Palestine beyond. This is now a closed military zone. The fortified medieval town of Atlit lay to the right, between the castle and the salt-pans, while the beach, also on the right, formed a rather exposed harbour.

**Crac des Chevaliers in the mid 13th century**
Much of what remains of Crac des Chevaliers today
is actually Mamluk, and dates from after the castle fell
to Sultan Baybars in 1271. This is certainly true of the
eastern side (1); this was the most vulnerable stretch of
wall, and most often damaged by sieges. The changes were
even more dramatic on the southern side (2), facing a
neighbouring hill across a deep fosse. This bore the brunt of
the final Mamluk attack; both its main rounded towers being so
damaged that they had to be rebuilt. In 1285 construction began on
a massive new rectangular tower, which today dominates this southern
wall. A stone aqueduct (2a) brought water from a tunnel in the hillside
into the internal moat. In contrast, the western wall (3), with its protruding
box machicolations (3a), overlooks a very steep valley and consists of
virtually unaltered Crusader work, as does the inner fortress; dating from
before 1170, it is protected by a moat (4a), a talus (4b), massive walls, and
towers built after Crac des Chevaliers had been handed over to the Hospitallers.

1

4a

2

2a

The picturesque Sea Castle at Sidon stands on a small rocky islet only a few metres from the shore. It was built in 1228 to protect the northern harbour of Sidon, which itself formed a vital stage in the sea route from Acre to western Europe. In the 13th century most ships hugged the coast and preferred to come ashore each night, which necessitated a chain of secure harbours. (Museum of the Order of St. John)

## Caesarea Maritima

Caesarea Maritima on the Palestinian coast boasts the best-preserved Crusader urban defences, largely because this site was abandoned for centuries after it had been retaken by the Mamluks. The main city gate was on its eastern side and had a drawbridge supported by a stone vault, which has been reconstructed. The lines of the town's fortifications follow those of the early medieval Islamic defences, though the walls themselves received their final form when Louis IX of France had the city refortified in 1252. The original height of this mid-13th-century wall is unknown, but in several places there were casemated arrow slits with sloping sills; the whole being fronted by a talus rising 8m from the base of a dry ditch 7–8m wide and 4–6m deep. The vertical counterscarp remains, along with 14 projecting towers. One tower on each of the landward sides of Caesarea had a bent entrance. The ruins of a castle were found on the southern harbour mole, consisting of a keep behind a wall with rectangular towers fronted by a sea-level rock-cut moat.

The mid 13th-century fortifications of Caesarea, as rebuilt by the Crusading King Louis IX of France, are the most complete examples of unaltered Crusader urban defences in the Middle East. (Duby Tal)

The excavated outer defences of Caesarea Maritima on the Palestinian coast clearly show how the moat of the refortified city followed the line of the wall precisely. The sloping lower part of the city wall is on the left while the near-vertical retaining wall of the moat is on the right.

# Arsuf

Archaeological investigations at Arsuf are much more recent and a great deal remains to be published. The site differed from that at Caesarea Maritima, as Arsuf takes advantage of a sandstone bluff overlooking a shallow natural haven near the modern Israeli town of Herzliya.

The city had reached its greatest extent during the pre-Islamic Byzantine period when it had an important Samaritan community, though not, it appears, a Jewish one. During the early Islamic period the extent, though not necessarily the population, of Arsuf was reduced, apparently in response to the threat of Byzantine naval attack. Arsuf was now, for the first time, given a fortified wall. This was the city that the Crusaders seized early in the 12th century, after which the conquerors continued to use the existing Islamic fortifications, restoring them and adding a new gate. During the early 13th century, the Crusaders added a castle on the edge of a cliff overlooking the sea. This included a courtyard surrounded by a high inner wall with two rectangular and four semicircular towers. An outer wall had five larger and lower bastions, the largest of which projected directly ahead of the twin gate-towers. This doubled-wall system was in turn surrounded by a deep moat strengthened by outer retaining walls forming a polygon. The seaward ends of this retaining system have, like much of the western side of the castle, collapsed as a result of cliff erosion.

A bridge on two piers led into the south-eastern side of the castle. It would originally have had a drawbridge into a short wall between the southern and easternmost outer towers. Some large circular structures in the north-eastern corner of the castle may have been ovens in a kitchen area, and on the western side was a polygonal keep over a vaulted hall. Much of the western side of the castle and all of its straight western wall have fallen down the cliff.

Although the Crusader military architects who designed the new fortifications of the town of Arsuf followed the lines of the existing Islamic defences, they added several much stronger walls and towers. Here the lower part of the south-eastern corner tower has been excavated, along with part of the moat and a retaining wall on the far right.

ABOVE LEFT Much of the ruins of the medieval Crusader city of Arsuf remains unexcavated, because the ground has been polluted by chemicals from an Israeli armaments factory. However, the foundations of the ruined east gate have been uncovered. Here the Crusaders followed the line of the previous Fatimid city fortifications, but added a stronger gate.

ABOVE RIGHT The northern part of the fosse, or moat, around the citadel at Arsuf. Massive strengthening piers were added to this, the longest stretch of outer retaining wall, probably because the pressure of loose sandy earth behind threatened to burst the wall and fill the moat.

RIGHT The rectangular area of very shallow water in the centre of this photograph is sheltered by the foundations of walls dating from the 13th-century Crusader occupation of Arsuf. It has sometime been interpreted as the remains of a small harbour, though it might also have been a wharf that was later flooded by a slight change in sea level. The massive pieces of masonry on the right are from the collapsed western side of the citadel overlooking this harbour or wharf.

At the base of this cliff was what some have identified as a harbour with jetties and corner towers. An alternative interpretation suggests that it included a flat area of land, just above sea level, which may have served as a wharf. A tunnel led from the fortress to the supposed 'port', perhaps as a final means of escape, while another tunnel led south from the courtyard into the moat. This could have served as a postern, enabling the garrison to attack an enemy in the moat.

# Life in the Holy Land castles

During the 13th century very few Crusader lords formed part of a village or rural community. Instead they lived in the cities where their way of life had more in common with the aristocratic elites of Italy than of France or Germany. Many members of the aristocracy no longer held much (or indeed any) land. Instead they maintained themselves by other forms of 'feudal rent'. Meanwhile the castles were under authority of professional chatelains. Most of the strategically significant castles were also passing into the hands of the Military Orders.

## Castles and social order

As in Italy, the knightly class of the Crusader States tried to preserve their social status and live what was seen as a knightly way of life. This did not mean that castles became mere fortresses garrisoned by low-status troops, whose comfort or cultural interests were neglected. Many castles provided a remarkably sophisticated and comfortable environment, no matter who actually lived in them. The remains of what would today be called 'Turkish baths' were found at Atlit and there may have been extensive gardens at Montfort. According to Willbrand of Oldenburg, the citadel of Beirut had mosaic floors that looked like gently rolling waves, while one room contained a fountain in the shape of a dragon. Even some smaller castles still contain traces of mosaics and painted plaster. Nevertheless, most of the sculptural decoration found at Safad dates from the 12th rather than the 13th century. It has also been assumed that the refined lifestyle seen in Crusader castles reflected Arab-Islamic and Byzantine cultural influences, and there is little reason to doubt this was true.

The most striking decoration was probably reserved for chapels, which included decorative stone panelling, floor mosaics and wall paintings. Here a distinctive style developed that was a mixture of western European and Byzantine artistic styles while including Islamic decorative elements. Quite a

Most of the wall-head defences and crenellations now visible on Crusader castles are either modern reconstructions or date from Mamluk rebuilding. However, aerial photographs from the early 20th century show that some of the original crenellations on the fortified church at Castel Blanc still existed at this time. They are seen here in greater detail. The upper gaps were for observation while the tapering slots at floor level were for shooting through.

Stone-carved heraldic shields bearing the coats-of-arms of rulers and other senior men decorated some Crusader fortifications, as was the case in western Europe. This carving of the arms of the Lusignan family was found in Acre. (Israel Antiquities Authority)

lot survives in castle chapels, though it is likely that wall paintings were also seen in other important parts of a castle.

The most detailed description of a seigneurial chapel was of that in the castle of Tyre, as rebuilt around 1212. It is found in an account of the assassination of Philip de Montfort, Lord of Tyre, in 1270. The killer had entered Philip's service and the murder took place when de Montfort was talking to some burgesses from Tyre in the outer lobby of the chapel. Another mass had started but as there were so few people in the chapel the assassin seized his opportunity and struck Philip with a dagger. He then attacked Philip's son John with a sword, but the youngster hid inside the altar, the front of which consisted of a wooden panel decorated with saints. The assassin's sword stuck in this panel, whereupon other people arrived and overpowered the killer. Philip, though mortally wounded, staggered to a stone bench in front of the entrance to his private chamber. Other evidence indicates that the chapel was probably at first-floor level, and had a staircase as well as a lobby. Castle chapels were often placed close to the lord's private rooms, not merely for convenience but because they also served as administrative meeting places.

Despite the Crusader States' loss of territory, castles and smaller fortifications continued to be centres of rural and agricultural administration, storage or distribution. More importantly they provided security, enabling agriculture to continue. Yet the poverty of so many of the 13th-century Crusader aristocracy meant that their garrisons were rarely as effective as those of the Military Orders, and even rulers were sometimes unable to pay or feed their own garrisons. This was particularly acute in the Principality of Antioch and the County of Tripoli, which rarely benefited from Papal appeals for money in support of the Kingdom of Jerusalem. Consequently it was common for garrisons to take part in agricultural to maintain themselves.

Amongst the smaller rural fortifications that continued to function was the Castle of Roger the Lombard in what is now Natanya. Caco, another rural fortification consisting of a tower and a reused Byzantine cistern, was not far away from this site. Khirbat Kurdana was different, consisting of a mill with a feeder dam and a defensive tower whose timber lower floor rested on stone corbels. It had one splayed arrow slit in the southern wall, and three in the north. During a second phase of construction after 1267, two floors were inserted on groin vaults, whose corner pilasters blocked three of the arrow slits. A large pointed arch on the west side was now defended by a box machicolation while the tower itself was flanked by two barrel-vaulted wheel chambers for a mill with a mill room above. These rural fortifications were small, but some others were more complex, including the Hospitaller castle of Coliat north of Tripoli.

Most cities and larger towns within the Crusader States had a castle as the residence of a ruler, his castellan or a local lord. By the mid 13th century the

King of Jerusalem's Seneschal had considerable authority over the royal fortresses, which played a significant role during the struggles between pro- and anti-Imperial factions for control of the dwindling Kingdom in the 1240s. The princely castles of Antioch and Tripoli were similarly under the authority of châtelains.

Apart from their military role protecting against invasion and during internal conflicts, the major castles were also used to receive important overseas visitors, as well as providing locations for politically significant weddings or festivals. Such events probably took place in their great halls and out of doors when weather permitted. They also served as courts of justice, and centres of administration and for the raising of taxes. High-status prisoners could normally expect to be held in such castles, though not necessarily in any comfort. In fact elite prisoners were sometimes kept in extremely poor conditions until they died, though others were treated with respect and consideration until release or ransom.

Another group of smaller fortifications were those of the competing Italian merchant republics: Pisa, Genoa, and Venice. These foreign powers had become significant landholders within the Crusader States, with the Venetians rivalling the King of Jerusalem as seigneurs around 13th-century Tyre. However, it was the great seaport of Acre that most concerned the Italians. Here considerable efforts were made, until the mid 13th century, to keep the quarters of the quarrelsome Italian merchant communes separated by neutral ground. Yet this did not stop the rivals from building ever taller towers for reasons of prestige as well as defence against rivals. The Pisans apparently had two such towers in their part of Acre during the first half of the 13th century. The Genoese, whose quarter was in the centre of Acre, had what was described as a 'great tower' called the Lamonçoia, until this was destroyed following Genoa's defeat by Venice and Pisa during the so-called War of St. Sabas. A Genoese 'new tower' mentioned 1249 may have been a replacement following the burning of the previous one. It was within crossbow range of the Pisan tower and, given the volatile relations between rival mercantile communes, Genoa not surprisingly sent military equipment from Italy to be used by their consul in Acre.

PAGE 42
### The city and citadel of Arsuf in the mid 13th century
Arsuf was a thriving commercial centre before the Crusaders arrived in 1101. It already had urban fortifications, but apparently lacked a citadel, though the remains of a small early Islamic tower may have been found beneath the castle added by the Crusaders in the early 13th century (1). During the Crusader occupation the existing Islamic urban defences were repaired and in the south-eastern corner these were greatly strengthened. A new city gate (2) was similarly built on the eastern side. The Crusader citadel (3) was an impressive structure consisting of a courtyard surrounded by a high inner wall with rectangular and semicircular towers (4). Massive outer bastions (5) were placed immediately in front of the inner towers. Beyond these was a deep fosse (6) surrounded by a carefully constructed retaining wall (7), needed because of the sandy nature of the soil. A drawbridge tower (8) provided access to the citadel. The city itself was protected by a wall with an outer fosse (9). The true nature of the 'harbour' at the base of the cliff (10) is still the subject of debate. Leased to the Hospitallers in 1261, the castle was considerably strengthened; yet Arsuf fell to the Mamluks only four years later. (After Roll and Smertenko, with additions by Nicolle)

PAGE 43
### The Templar stables in the city of Atlit, 13th century
The extensive stables that were built against the southern wall of Atlit were not reused after the fortified city was destroyed by the Mamluks in 1265. This reconstruction attempts to illustrate one corner of the Templars' stable area next to the southern city gate of Atlit town, as it probably looked early in the 13th century before various modifications were undertaken; a section of the stable walls has been removed in the illustration. The whole area contained permanent stabling for over 200 animals, including war-horses, smaller horses for turcopole cavalry or to be used as baggage animals, plus draught oxen and even camels. Oxen seem to have fed from continuous troughs, whereas horse-troughs or mangers were usually divided into individual sections. There were also wells, drainage systems, grain chutes, tethering points and rooms that might have served as storage, offices or accommodation.

10

1

7

6

3

4

8

5

9

2

For caption see page 41

The Templar stables in the city of Atlit, 13th century

For caption see page 41

# Religious centres and the Holy Orders

Relatively few fortifications were built specifically to protect religious centres. Of these Jerusalem was the most important, and during the 15 years when it was again under Crusader control, efforts were made to restore some defences. The city walls had been dismantled by Saladin, but a barbican in front of St. Stephen's Gate was repaired, along with the Citadel, whose existing glacis may date from this period. However, there is some argument over where a castle constructed in 1240 was located. Some historians believe it was next to what was then called the Gaza Gate, where the Tower of the Maidens and the Tower of the Hospital were sited, but others maintain that the castle of 1240 was at the north-western corner of the Old City. Other fortifications were sited in an attempt to encourage the development of specific locations as centres of pilgrimage. However, by the 13th century security had deteriorated to such an extent that local bishops would evacuate threatened towns for the relative safety of these nearby fortresses.

The most significant 'religious' fortifications were, of course, those of the Military Orders. These included towns that were under an Order's control. In such places the citadel would normally be used as the Order's local headquarters. In Acre, however, the headquarters of the Hospitallers and of the Templars formed separate enclaves, each capable of individual defence.

Elsewhere the Military Orders had become substantial landholders and the territory under their control was the best defended in the Crusader States. The Templars, for example, were in the process of forming a sort of autonomous palatinate around Tartus by the mid 12th century, just as the Hospitallers would do around Crac des Chevaliers. Within this expanding Templar palatinate, the castle of Castel Blanc was an impressive *église donjon* (fortified church) that dominated the surrounding castle. It was built in the final quarter of the 12th century but was subsequently repaired extensively. Access from the ground-floor church to the upper chamber and roof is so awkward that the building cannot have been permanently garrisoned. However, it was very defensible and had a slit machicolation over the main church door.

In 1217–18 the Templars demolished the late-12th-century fort of Le Destroit and replaced it with the much larger castle of Atlit. The latter was largely built with pilgrim manpower, and became known as Château Pelerin. It was so strong that it survived the fall of Atlit town in 1265 and was only abandoned in August 1291, after the fall of Acre itself. A variation on the way Crusader builders reused ancient materials occurred in 1218, when the Templars cut a moat across the narrow isthmus at Atlit. They not only found ancient walls, which offered a ready supply of cut stones, but also gold coins with which they paid their workers!

During the 1920s, when this photograph was taken, the eastern end of the hilltop of Safita was largely devoid of buildings except for the remains of a tall gate, here seen on the right. Behind it rose the stern rectangular fortified church that the Crusaders called Castel Blanc. Today this, like the rest of the hill, is almost entirely covered with attractive stone houses, many made from masonry from the collapsed outer fortifications of the Crusader castle.

The town that was later built outside Atlit castle was defended by much weaker fortifications, although the huge stables were very impressive. These seem to have been based upon the traditional design of an Islamic *khan*, or protected lodging place, for merchants. Here archaeologists found evidence for the everyday working life of a garrison, including tethering points and sockets for halter-rings for animals, and a courtyard well with a drain leading outside the buildings. The flat roofs that covered this remarkably large area rested on piers and wooden beams and consisted of boards. A concrete crust consisted of gravel and lime, rendered smooth with lime plaster, just as in traditional Palestinian domestic architecture. Most of the timber came from Mount Carmel, though some fragments of cedar were also found in the ruins, possibly shipped in from Lebanon or Cyprus.

The south-western corner tower of the inner defences of Castel Blanc, now called Safita.

The Atlit garrison relied on shallow dug wells, which produced slightly brackish but drinkable water, and one well in the middle of the stable yard remained in use until modern times. Other neighbouring buildings were not linked to the interior of the main stable structure but were accessed from the beach. The northern gateway of the complex was intended for heavier traffic than the other entrances, and had a roadway paved with diagonal slabs. The impressive door was approached by a metalled slope and seems to have been the only entrance to the main stable yard. Carts probably remained outside in a shaded area or shed. Stone 'grain chutes' made it easier to get the grain into various storage bins. Other rooms were possibly used as stores for the harnesses. However, only one room was specifically designed for larger horses, presumably the war-horses of the Brother Knights. It had sufficient space for animals to lie down, perhaps in separate wooden stalls.

Meanwhile, the grooms were provided with comfortable living quarters next to the stables. Much broken pottery was found here along with a steel 'striker' to be used with flint and tinder to start a cooking fire, while their drinking water was cooled in the semi-porous jars which remain traditional throughout much of the Middle East. Most of the ceramics were locally made, though some finer ware had been imported from Cyprus or Italy. A blacksmith also worked somewhere around the site, though the exact spot could not be identified.

The castellans of the main Hospitaller castles were under the authority of the Marshal. In peacetime the 'Castellans of Syria' answered to the Marshal and to the Chapter General of the Order, though in time of war the Marshal's authority was more direct, particularly if he was personally present within their bailiwick, or district. However, some smaller castles may not have had castellans and were instead garrisoned by mercenaries.

With regard to the number of personnel present in each castle, the evidence can be confusing. Eighty Hospitaller brethren were said to have been killed or captured when Arsuf fell to the Mamluks in 1265, whereas the complete garrison totalled around 1,000 men. Fifteen years later the Hospitallers were said to have had 600 cavalry in Margat, whereas a source from 1211 indicated that the complete garrison consisted of 2,000 men. In 1255 a Papal document maintained that the Order had only 60 mounted troops in Crac des Chevaliers, and proposed stationing 40 more in a new castle to be built on Mount Tabor. To further confuse the issue, a letter from the Hospitaller Grand Master, written in 1268, stated that the Order had only 300 brethren in the whole of Syria, so it is clearly impossible to present firm figures for the garrisons of specific castles.

The lower part of the great fortified tower that rises over Safita (Castel Blanc) consisted of a church, which has remained to this day throughout the tumultuous history of Syria. The impact of earthquakes, which still sometimes rock this region, can be seen in the cracked semi-dome of the apse.

### The fortified church and town of Safita (Castel Blanc) in the mid 13th century

The great tower or keep (1) of Castel Blanc in the Syrian coastal mountains was a massively fortified church rather than simply a castle. The lower chamber (2) formed the church with a semi-domed apse at its eastern end (3); a function which continues to this day. The upper chamber (4) consists of a two-aisled hall supported by three columns. Access to this upper chamber from the church was within the south-western corner (5) and was not particularly convenient for military purposes, while access to the roof was by stairs against the western wall of the upper chamber. A rock-cut cistern lay beneath the church

(6). An extensive platform surrounds the church, and appears to have had a defensive wall which formed an inner enceinte (7). Apart from the platform, the only substantial surviving element of these inner defences is the small south-western tower (8). Even less remains of the outer fortifications of Castel Blanc, recreated in the lower illustration, with the notable exception of part of a great entrance tower on the eastern side of the hill (9). Photographs taken before the modern village of Safita expanded into a small but thriving town, indicate that this formed only part of a complex of fortifications around the entrance to the Crusader town.

**The fortified church and town of Safita (Castel Blanc)
in the mid 13th century**

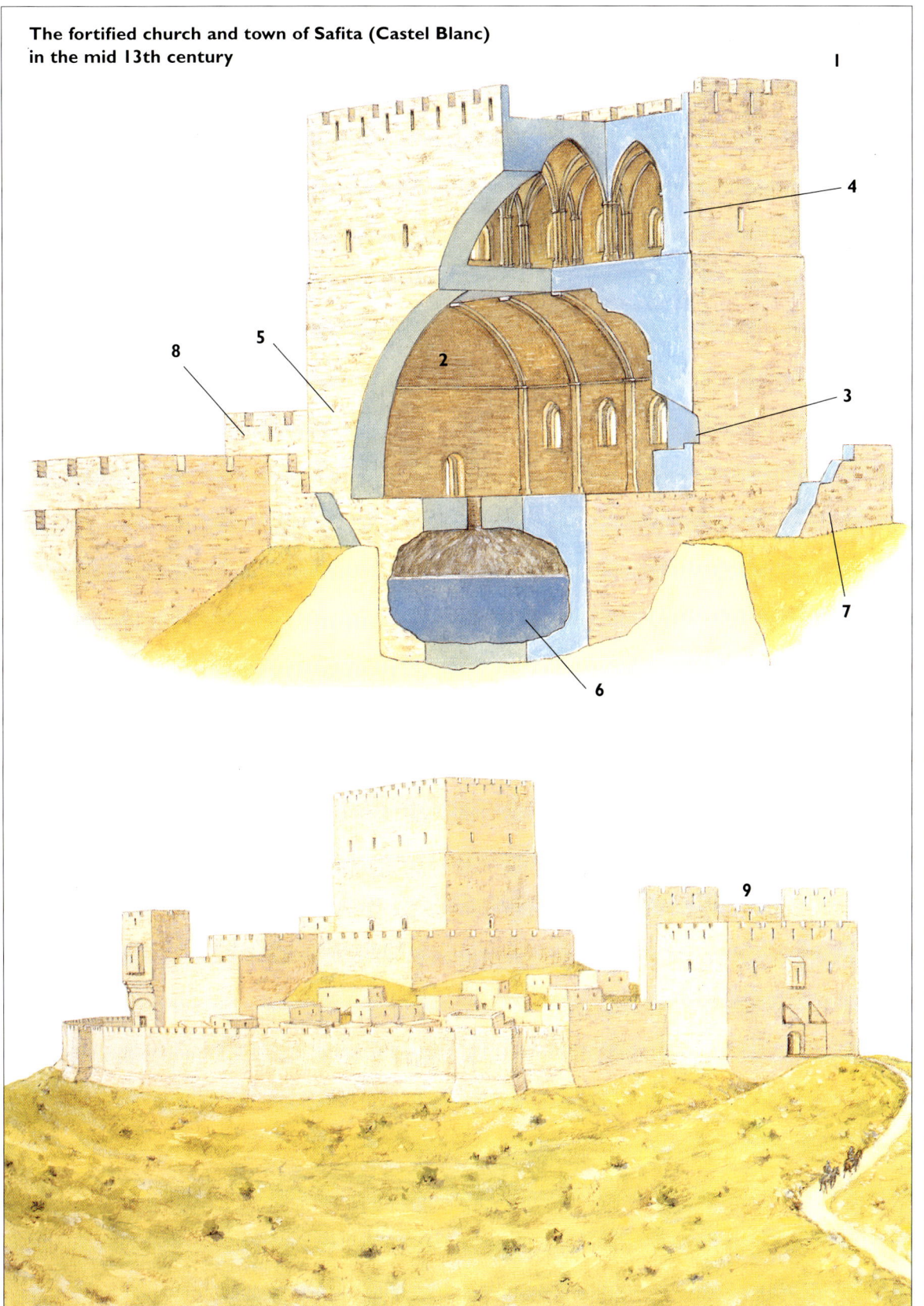

# The Teutonic Knights

The Teutonic Knights possessed several important fortresses in the Middle East. These included Montfort in Galilee, which had a separate hall, built in the second quarter of the 13th century next to the Wadi al-Qarn. It stands north of the castle, at the bottom of a steep slope. The hall is a rectangular structure, 40m x 10–12m, over a barrel-vaulted undercroft. It was probably constructed in at least two stages and is attached to a dam across the wadi; this dam having sluices to control the flow of water. Part of the structure originally served as a mill, probably for processing sugar cane, where a horizontal millwheel seems to have been powered by water directed through wooden channels. The main hall above could not have been used for storing food as it was in a vulnerable position outside the castle. So perhaps the undercroft served as a stable or kitchen after the upper hall was added; the whole structure then forming a guesthouse for high-ranking visitors to the Teutonic Knights' castle. During the final phase of the Crusader occupation of Montfort, a *faubourg*, or suburb, may also have grown up outside the castle.

The first castle donated to the Teutonic Knights in Cilicia was at Amoude, which was handed over by the Armenian King in 1212. Situated on a rocky outcrop in the middle of the Cilician plain, it was a simple fortified enclosure to which the Teutonic Knights added a three-storey keep. Another possible reason for the selection of Amoude was the abundant availability of fish from the nearby Ceyhan River; this still clearly being the case when the German traveller Willbrand of Oldenburg visited Amoude some years later.

BELOW LEFT Montfort in northern Galilee was a typical and very dramatic spur castle, located on an easily defensible extension of one of the surrounding hills. This position was further strengthened by the excavation of dry ditches, or fosses, separating the castle from the main hill. The Crusader fortifications of Montfort all date from the 13th century and the place served as the Headquarters of the Order of Teutonic Knights until it fell to the Mamluks in 1271. (Duby Tal)

BELOW RIGHT The castle of Montfort: 1 – outer ward; 2 – upper castle; 3 – donjon built over a large cistern; 4 – fosse; 5 – presumed 'guest house' built on earlier mill; 6 – remains of a dam across the Wadi al-Qarn. (After Dean, Hubatsch, Frankel and Pringle)

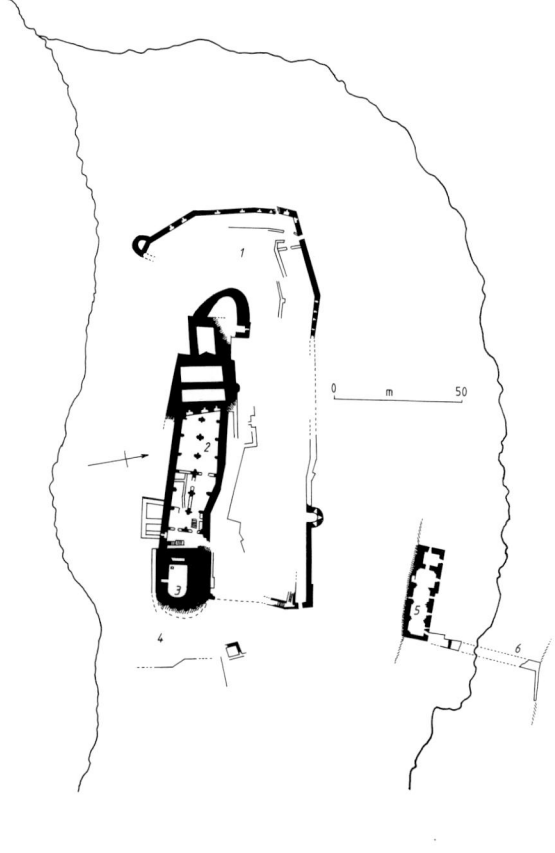

# The Crusader States at war

Despite the development of larger transport ships and better accommodation for horses on board, the Crusader States continued to suffer from a serious shortage of livestock. This not only applied to large war-horses but also to pack animals. The limited territory of the remaining Crusader States also meant that they lacked pasture to maintain large herds. The shortage had several effects, not least of which was to make it difficult for armies to move around between their main fortified centres. Furthermore, huge efforts were made to avoid losses of horses on campaign or in battle. In complete contrast, the Crusaders' Muslim neighbours had access to very large numbers of horses, though more so in Syria than in Egypt. These not only included the relatively small horses traditionally associated with Turkish horse-archers, but also the large, finely bred and hot-blooded mounts used by elite armoured cavalry.

Given such constraints, it is hardly surprising that the Crusader States – and even those new Crusader forces arriving from Europe – relied on fortifications to an ever increasing extent. Furthermore, castles played a leading role in the Crusaders' rare attempts to regain lost territory. Sometimes land was temporarily abandoned as a result of the enemy's raiding expeditions, which often meant that villages and even towns had to be evacuated. Sometimes Islamic armies attempted to destroy such places, although small-scale raids merely damaged crops, orchards, vineyards, olive groves and other agricultural targets. The destruction of food stores and economic assets, like mills, would be considered a significant success, so the Crusader States placed great emphasis on giving them some degree of fortification. If this failed, the damaged facilities might hopefully be regained, repaired and refortified, as happened to the mills at Recordane during the 13th century.

Meanwhile the fortified cities served as centres from which such localised reconquests could be launched. The citadels built at Jaffa, Caesarea and Sidon by Emperor Frederick II as nominal ruler of the Kingdom of Jerusalem, may have provided secure bases for such limited operations. Certainly the Kingdom of Jerusalem made what were, in the circumstances of the time, considerable efforts to re-establish control over the southern coast of Lebanon in 1227–28, during which period the Sea Castle of Sidon was constructed on a previously uninhabited coastal islet. Only later were serious fortifications added to the town of Sidon itself, which thereafter remained under Crusader control until its evacuation in 1291.

Safad castle, lost to Saladin in 1188, returned to Crusader hands from 1218 to 1220 when it was apparently intended as a base from which to reconquer Galilee. As a result, when the Muslims took it again in 1220, they completely dismantled the existing castle. Safad was handed back to the Kingdom of Jerusalem in 1240, whereupon major efforts were made to refortify it, probably for the same strategic reasons. A few years later the Crusading King Louis IX of France camped as close as possible to Frederick's fortifications at Jaffa, in order to protect the building of a stronger city wall. Louis probably did something similar at Sidon where an apparent hall along the northern face of the Sea Castle served as his headquarters.

However, such rebuilding efforts did not always succeed. For example, the Fifth Crusade, using Acre as its base, failed to retake Mount Tabor in 1217, although the latter was closer to Acre than to any comparable Islamic seat of power. Several efforts launched from Antioch after 1191 similarly failed to regain territory lost by the Principality. The main reason for these uncertain results was the Crusader States' lack of sufficient manpower to undertake proper siege operations. Consequently they largely relied on raiding tactics, and these could only regain territory if an enemy was willing to relinquish it. Full-scale offensives were only possible when large Crusading armies arrived from western Europe, and these were few and not always successful.

Meanwhile the upgrading or repair of existing fortifications was essentially defensive. Even the decision to refortify Ascalon in 1239 was initially defensive, to face any threat from Egyptian-held Gaza while the Crusaders planned to attack Damascus. In the event they attacked the Egyptians instead, and suffered catastrophic defeat at the battle of La Forbie in 1244. Thereupon Egyptian forces blockaded Ascalon until it surrendered.

The County of Tripoli enjoyed a better strategic situation, and although it lost some territory to Saladin and his successors, its heartland in what are now northern Lebanon and the southern part of the Syrian coast was strongly protected by the Military Orders. In fact this territory remained a substantial and well-fortified base area from which Crusader forces could raid their Muslim neighbours. This caused massive economic damage and kept the Arab villages so subdued that many accepted Crusader *suzereinty*, even within rugged and inaccessible mountain regions. Hospitaller garrisons from Crac des Chevaliers and Margat often joined forces to raid the hinterland of Hama and other nearby Islamic cities, and the strength of the Hospitaller palatinate in the north of the County of Tripoli even obliged the fearsome Isma'ili 'Assassins' to pay tribute. This tribute only ended with the fall of Crac des Chevaliers to the Mamluks. Even then, some remaining Crusader garrisons remained strong enough to launch further raids; in 1280, 200 knights attacked the fertile Buqai'ah plain near Crac, despite the fact that the latter fortress was now in Islamic hands.

Things seemed quieter in the now tiny Principality of Antioch. However, several Crusader-held ports were already being used as bases from which to launch naval raids against Islamic coasts and shipping. This might be interpreted as 'the wave of the future' in the struggle between Christian and Islamic forces in the Middle East and eastern Mediterranean, something which became a major aspect of 14th-century warfare.

The only large-scale or strategic Crusading expeditions in the Middle East during the 13th century were those launched against Egypt, which was now the centre of regional Islamic power. One of these seaborne invasions provides the only known evidence for a classic motte-style castle from this period. When the Fifth Crusade landed on the western bank of the main eastern Delta branch of the Nile, facing Damietta, on May 27, 1218, they fortified their camp with the usual ditch and rampart. The campaign dragged on through the summer

### The fall of Arsuf, 1265

The relatively new citadel of Arsuf was leased to the Military Order of the Hospitallers by the once-powerful Ibelin family in 1261. The Hospitallers then poured money, materials and effort into strengthening this vital fortification, which formed one of the southernmost coastal outposts of the Crusader Kingdom of Jerusalem. Nevertheless, only four years later, the powerful Mamluk Sultanate of Egypt and Syria launched a major offensive under Sultan Baybars, who was one of the most effective military leaders in medieval history. In fact Baybars pretended to be on a hunting expedition in what is now the occupied West Bank when he and his troops swooped. First they attacked Caesarea, which fell after only a week. Haifa was then destroyed, but Atlit held out,

and so Baybars besieged Arsuf. Despite its Hospitaller garrison, which included 270 knights, the town fell and the citadel capitulated only three days later. Archaeological evidence of this final siege includes not only a thick layer of ash but also an extraordinary number of mangonel stones. Those of the Crusader defenders were mostly found in neat piles, never having been shot. Those of the Mamluks, however, not only included chipped and broken examples of the carefully carved and balanced missiles preferred by mangonel operators, but also large numbers of more roughly shaped rocks. This seems to indicate that the Mamluks launched such a massive bombardment that they ran out of ammunition and had to collect whatever stones were suitable from the neighbouring hills. (After Roll and Smertenko, with additions by Nicolle)

The fall of Arsuf, 1265

and autumn, despite the capture of the Chain Tower of Damietta. Operations stagnated during winter when the Crusader army was virtually trapped within its fortified camp on the western bank of the river. However, Damietta finally capitulated in 1219. The Crusaders then seized the fortified town of Tanis. According to James de Vitry, who was eyewitness, the Crusaders built a third fortification in the middle of Lake Manzala, between Damietta and Tanis.

This was followed by a new and separate fourth construction on the west bank facing Damietta. It was on a sort of motte, which, according to de Vity, was:

> 'raised on the height of a mound until it resembled a hill, enclosing the sand with a wall of clayey soil, for in Egypt stones are not to be found unless they are carried with great labour from Cyprus or Syria (by ship) … In the middle they erected a wooden tower of astonishing height, not only for the defence of the castle, but also so that from a distance it might appear as a beacon to those sailing to Damietta.'

Apparently this unusual castle consisted of a mound of sand retained by a clay ringwork with a timber tower on top. The design may have been determined by a lack of building stone in this part of Egypt, where traditional Nile Delta architecture was of brick. However, it is interesting to note the major role played by Germans and Frisians who provided the timber, and the fact that the majority of men on this Crusade came from areas of western Europe where the old motte style of castle remained common.

The defensive function of Crusader fortifications is obvious but the precise way in which they operated during the 13th century is not always clear. The many small towers that dotted Crusader territory may, for example, have served as observation posts and local refuges. Nevertheless, warning of the approach of enemy forces did not necessitate fortifications, however small, so perhaps their tiny garrisons were expected to offer suicidal resistance in the

(1) The castle of Belfort (structures built by the Lords of Sagette 1139–90 are hatched, Ayyubid structures 1190–1240 are stippled, Templar structures are black, and Mamluk and Ottoman structures are unshaded):
1 – early Mamluk residential tower;
2 – Ayyubid great tower;
3 – early Mamluk casemates;
4 – early Mamluk postern;
5 – early Mamluk salient with two towers;
6 – Templar chapel;
7 – 12th-century Crusader donjon;
8 – 17th-century Ottoman buildings;
9 – 12th-century Crusader main wall;
10 – early Mamluk entrance way;
11 – early Mamluk entrance passage;
12 – early Mamluk entrance ramp;
13 – early Mamluk hall.
(After Corvisier)

(2) The castle of Margat:
1 – north-western great tower;
2 – outer fosse;
3 – outer enclosure wall;
4 – inner enclosure wall;
5 – outer entrance tower;
6 – forecourt between outer and inner gates;
7 – inner gate;
8 – substructure of vaulted chapter house;
9 – magazine chambers;
10 – chapel;
11 – two-storied hall;
12 – southern great tower rebuilt by the Mamluks;
13 – hall;
14 – open cistern.
(After Müller-Wiener)

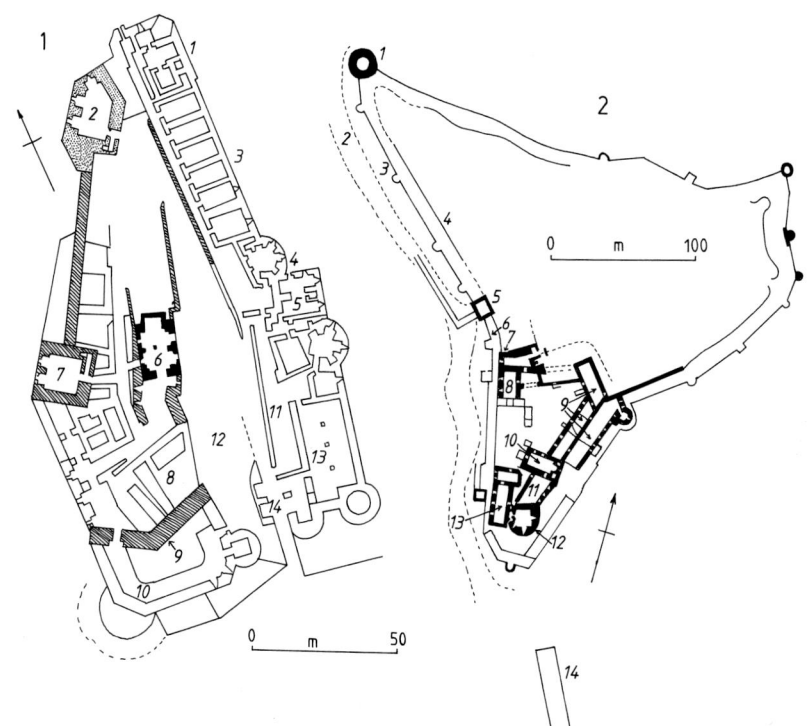

hope of delaying an attack upon a major centre. Delays or truces clearly featured prominently in resistance. A short three months truce with Saladin, after the Battle of Hattin, enabled Renaud de Sagette to prepare his castle of Belfort for a prolonged siege. Chroniclers refer to supplies being sent, and to the repair of its walls and gate. Yet when the crisis came, Belfort fell quite easily. The importance of outlying castles was clearly not lost on Saladin, whose biographer Imad al-Din wrote of Antioch after Hattin that 'To take away her fortresses is to take away her life.'

Good visibility was important for a major fortress. A sentry on the inner towers of Atlit, for example, was said to have been able to see an approaching enemy 13km away, but this was merely a result of its coastal location. Furthermore the site of Atlit could, to some extent, 'control' movement along the vital coastal road. At one time the selection of the site of Amoude in Cilicia as the location for a Teutonic Knights castle was thought to reflect the amount of land beneath its gaze. More importantly the hill of Amoude lay close to a strategic river crossing located in the heart of a fertile and densely populated plain. One of the Teutonic Knights' other important castles in the Kingdom of Cilician Armenia was Haruniya, close to a very important pass through the Amanus Mountains linking Cilicia and the plains of northern Syria. Such considerations were far more important than the distance that could be surveyed from the highest towers.

Despite the development of more powerful siege machines, most notably the counterweight trebuchet, the basic techniques of siege warfare remained the same as they had been during the 12th century. This was as true for the defenders as for the attackers. Given their numerical weakness, the basic strategy adopted by Crusader garrisons when facing a major assault was to retire into their citadel until the raiders hopefully withdrew. For several decades this worked well, especially against ill-disciplined foes like the Khwarawzians, who were themselves little more than a 'refugee army' fleeing ahead of Genghis Khan's more determined forces.

Clearly the construction of powerful defences made the Islamic states consider smaller campaigns as little more than pointless. Major invasions now had to be conducted by sizeable forces and even the hugely powerful Mamluk

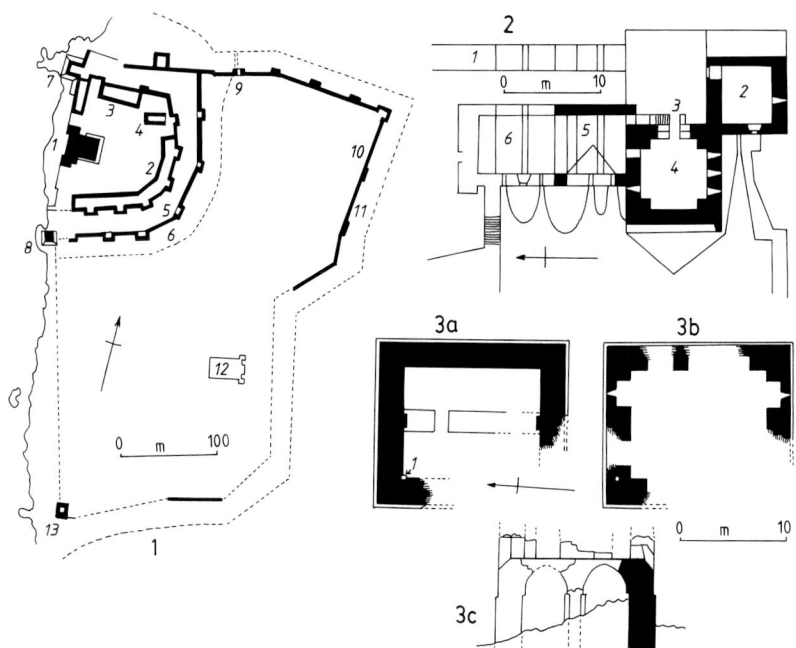

(1) Tartus:
1 – donjon;
2 – inner wall of the citadel;
3 – banqueting hall;
4 – chapel;
5 – outer citadel wall;
6 – inner fosse;
7 – north-western tower;
8 – south-western tower of the citadel;
9 – north gate of the city;
10 – city wall;
11 – city fosse;
12 – Cathedral of Our Lady of Tortosa;
13 – south-western corner tower of city walls.
(After Deschamps and Müller-Wiener)

(2) The fortified mill at Recordane (Khirbat Kardanah):
1 – bridge across the stream;
2 – first mill;
3 – entrance to the tower protected by a machicolation;
4 – fortified tower;
5 – second and third mills;
6 – fourth and fifth mills added during the Ottoman period. (After Pease)

(3a–c) Remains of the fortified tower of Caco (al-Qaqun): 3a – lower floor or basement with ceramic drainage pipe (1) from the roof; 3b – upper floor with pipe embedded within the corner wall; 3c – east–west section through the existing structure. (After Leach)

Sultanate of Egypt and Syria could not take all fortified places in a single campaign. Indeed some of the strongest Crusader fortresses were left until last. Furthermore, the Mamluks had to take complete control of major citadels if they wanted to occupy a city or region permanently. The fact that it took the Mamluks over 40 years to subdue what looked like small, isolated, vulnerable and demoralised coastal enclaves demonstrates the soundness of the Crusader States' defensive strategy. That it ultimately failed was a reflection of geopolitical factors, not of the defences, their garrisons or their tactics.

The more warning a garrison received of an impending attack, the better its chances of a successful defence. Yet Crusader garrisons often had little warning. Sultan Baybars, for example, was famous for the care he took to achieve surprise, sometimes not even informing his senior commanders of the real destination of a raid or siege campaign until his army was already on the march. This forced the Crusader States to spread their defences amongst several potential targets, further contributing to the remarkably small size of some garrisons.

Larger towns and cities could summon local militias when threatened, and such communal forces were recorded even before the emergence of real 'communes' with Crusader cities. At the same time major urban centres like Acre housed relatively large professional forces, yet their effectiveness was not guaranteed; Antioch capitulated in 1268 after a siege of only five days, despite being fully garrisoned.

The large numbers that crowded into a city or its citadel as the outer town and suburbs were abandoned to the enemy must have caused problems. There would have been far more frightened mouths to feed and only a small proportion of such refugees would have been effective fighting men. The final defence of Acre in 1291 drew in many available troops from other coastal enclaves, weakening them to such an extent that, after Acre fell, most other outposts simply surrendered.

When such a city fell much of its population is unlikely to have been able to escape, especially when disciplined and organised conquerors, like the Mamluks, placed guards on the gates to avoid unauthorised looting by their own men. Even on the coast there were not enough ships for everybody to escape. As a result many of the poor, unable to pay for a passage in such ships, with nowhere to go and no family links outside the Crusader States, had no alternative but to remain. A larger number of these usually unrecorded 'poor' were presumably absorbed into what became the Arab-speaking coastal populations of Syria, Lebanon and Palestine.

Although the basic techniques of siege warfare remained largely unchanged, more powerful artillery was now available in increasing numbers. The mining operations that had proved so effective against Crusader fortifications in the 12th century continued, but were now supported by massed trebuchets. This combination proved highly effective against Crac des Chevaliers in 1271. The demoralisation of Crusader garrisons during these final decades may have been overstated, but constant bombardment by great rocks clearly had an impact that was probably more significant than the physical damage caused.

On the other side, the defenders' use of espringals and 'great crossbows' could prove very effective, because the attackers were more exposed to the massive arrows shot by such weapons than the defenders within their stone walls. 'Great crossbows' were used by the Templars of Atlit in 1220, causing such heavy casualties that the Ayyubid Sultan al-Muazzam withdrew his army. The Templar garrison of Jaffa used the same sort of weapons in defence of Jaffa in 1266.

Other chroniclers add further details about defensive measures; these being particularly abundant in accounts of the final siege of Acre in 1291. For example, Oliver of Paderborn, in his *Historia Damiatina*, described one tower as having huge iron spikes attached to wooden hoardings. Similar obstacles may have been planted in the moat. However, a suggestion that, during the final epic siege, the main wall of Acre was protected by wooden barbicans seems more doubtful.

# The fate of the fortifications

The speed of the collapse of the Crusader-held enclaves along the eastern Mediterranean coast came as a shock to Catholic Christian Europe. This was all the more painful because so much effort and expense had been put into their fortifications. Yet despite the impressive nature of some castles and urban defences, their subsequent fate depended upon their location rather than their strength. In general, those on the coast were demolished and abandoned by the Mamluks whereas many of those sited inland, especially overlooking strategically important passes, continued to be used. In many cases the latter were then considerably strengthened.

Despite several exceptions, the one feature that seems to have been consistent in Mamluk strategy was that the Muslim conquerors demolished those places they felt unable to garrison adequately, and which could become the targets of Crusader counter-attacks. If a castle was more vulnerable than useful, it was destroyed. On the other hand, the new Mamluk rulers seem to have tried to maintain existing western European forms of land tenure and peasant servitude, which had proved very effective in supporting the Crusader military elite. Unfortunately – from the Mamluks' point of view – this was not practical, as under Islamic law it was illegal to enslave fellow Muslims, even the poorest peasants, or tie them to land as serfs.

The fate of Jerusalem, as an important (though small) inland city, was less clear cut. Most Crusader fortifications here were broken down though not entirely demolished, with the exception of the Tower of David citadel. Here the

The Burj al-Hazna or Treasury Tower stands next to the north-eastern corner of the Hospitaller fortified convent in Acre. Its foundations are on one of the biggest towers of what had been the northern wall of the city. Beyond this the new suburb of Montmussard was fortified during the 13th century. The Hospitaller Convent, also known as the Citadel, is behind the high wall on the left.

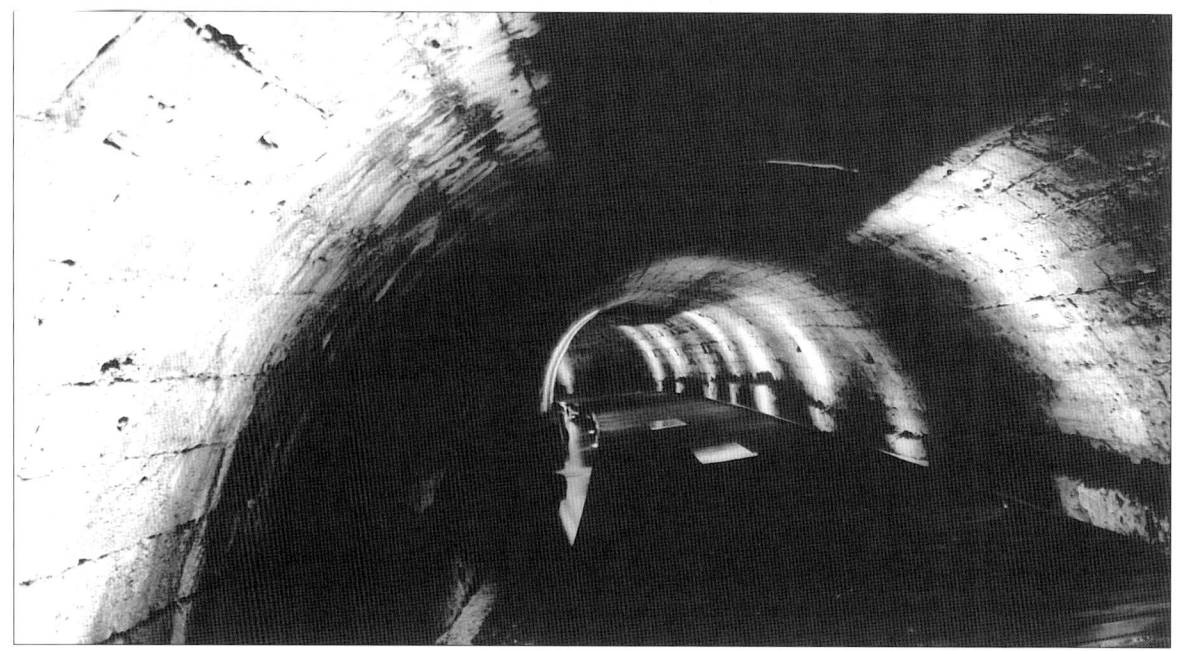

When archaeologists found this remarkable stone-lined tunnel beneath the old city of Acre, it was filled with rubble to within less than a metre of the roof. Once cleared, however, it proved to be a large structure linking the centre of the city with the area of what had been the Templar castle in the south-western corner of Acre. Though not 'secret' in any real sense of the word, the tunnel was probably private.

lower parts of the Crusader structure remained largely intact, including the glacis, while the main tower above was rebuilt as the Mamluk garrison's only strong fortification within the city. The 12th-century fortresses in what is now southern Jordan had already been strengthened by the Ayyubids (see Fortress 21: *Crusader Castles in the Holy Land 1097–1192*), and this process continued under the Mamluk rulers from the mid 13th to the end of the 15th century. A comparable process was seen in the coastal mountains of Syria where archaeologists have found that more of the famous 'Crusader castle' of Crac des Chevaliers is actually of Mamluk construction. The same has been found at Belfort in southern Lebanon.

Down on the coast of Palestine, the citadel of Arsuf was rased by the Mamluks after its capture in 1265, never to be used again except for a brief period during the First World War when British troops established a strongpoint in its ruins. After Tripoli fell to the Mamluks, its new rulers largely abandoned the Crusader coastal city, which declined into the small fishing port of al-Mina. Only later did the Mamluks build some coastal towers to guard the port. Meanwhile, a new Islamic town developed around the Crusader Castle of St. Giles, as it was widely known, which was on a steep hill a few kilometres inland. This became modern Tripoli.

There is a joke amongst scholars specialising in medieval Middle Eastern fortifications that the great Mamluk Sultan Baybars was 'a great builder of Crusader castles'. A similarity in military building techniques on both sides of the Crusader–Saracen frontier still causes problems when it comes to identifying who exactly built what. There was certainly a flow of technical and stylistic ideas in both directions, but it is often difficult to state who were the instigators of new ideas or the most original developments. What is clear is that during the Crusader period the Middle East served as an important centre for the dissemination of developments within the art of fortification, and did so in all directions. Those directly responsible for transmitting such ideas could range from humble Italian sailors to the Grand Masters of the Military Orders. Amongst the latter, Hermann von Salza, Grand Master of the Teutonic Knights, is credited with bringing new concepts of castle design from the Middle East to the rather backward province of Thuringia in Germany. He is unlikely to have been alone.

# Visiting the fortifications today

The names given to cities, castles, villages and practically every other feature of the Middle Eastern landscape have changed over the centuries. Furthermore, they were known by different names by different peoples during the period of the Crusades. The list of alternative names given below includes most of the sites mentioned in this book, but Turkish and Hebrew names only apply to locations that lie within the modern states of Turkey or Israel. Cities that are commonly known by variations of their correct or ancient names are given these within the text. This is not, however, a full list of sites fortified by the Crusaders during the 13th century.

| Medieval French or Latin | Arabic | Turkish or Hebrew | Medieval French or Latin | Arabic | Turkish or Hebrew |
|---|---|---|---|---|---|
| Alexandretta | Iskandariyah | Iskerderun | Coliat | al-Qulai'ah | |
| Amoude | Khan 'Amudah | Amuda | Crac des Chevaliers | Hisn al-Akrad | |
| Aradus | Ruad or Arwad | | Cursat | Qusair | |
| Arima | al-Araymah | | Gaston | Baghras | Bagra |
| Arsur (Apollonia) | Arsuf | | Gibelcar | 'Akkar (Jabal 'Akkar) | |
| Belfort (or Beaufort) | Shaqif Arnun (or Qal'at al-Shaqif) | | Gibelet (or Byblos) | Jbayl | |
| | | | Judin | Qal'at Jiddin | |
| Belhacem | Qal'at Abu'l-Hasan | | La Tor de l'Opital | Burj al-Shamali | |
| Botron (or Le Boutron) | al-Batrun | | Le Destroit | Qal'at Dustray | |
| | | | Maraclea | Maraqiyah | |
| Caco | al-Qaqun | | Margat | al-Marqab | |
| Caesarea | al-Qaisariyah | Sedot Yam | Mirabel | | Migdal Afeq |
| Cafarlet | Kfar Lam | Habonim | Montfort | Qal'at al-Qurayn | |
| Calansue | al-Qalansuwa | | Nephin | Anafah | |
| Casal des Plains | | Azor | Recordane | Khirbat Kardanah | |
| Casal Imbert | al-Zib | Akhziv | Roche de Roussel | Hajar Shuglan | Chilvan Kale |
| Castel Blanc | Burj Safitha | | Saphet | Safad | Zefat |
| Castel Neuf | Hunin | | St. Simeon | | Süveydiye |
| Castel Rouge | al-Qalat Yahmur | | Tortosa | Tartus | |
| Castellum Regis | al-Mi'ilyah | Ma'alot | Trapesac | Darbsak | |
| Caymont | Tal Qaimun | Yoqne'am | Turris Salinarum | Tal Tananim | |
| Château Pelerin | Atlit | | Villejargon | 'Arqah | |

On the mainland next to the castle of Atlit is one of the rarest sights in the Middle East: a largely undisturbed Crusader cemetery. Some of the most decorated gravestones have been removed, and most that remain are quite plain. However, amongst them are a few with carved crosses. The identities of those buried beneath are unknown but they may have been senior members of the Hospitaller garrison.

# Syria

Generally, the 13th-century Crusader castles of Syria are easier to access. The largest and most dramatic remain Margat (Marqab) and Crac des Chevaliers (Hisn al-Akrad), both of which have been opened for tourists. Both have substantial later Islamic additions and neither has been spoiled by over-restoration. South of Margat, the historic port city of Tartus contains several Crusader buildings and fortifications, some of which are still inhabited by local people. The tiny island of Arwad, a few minutes journey in an open boat from Tartus, still has a fort dating from the Crusader period and – perhaps more importantly – also has some of the best fish restaurants in Syria.

RIGHT Castel Rouge, or Qal'at Yahmur as it is now called, is one of the smallest, most complete and most picturesque Crusader castles in Syria. It is unusual in still being inhabited by a family from the surrounding village. The inner tower or keep measures 14m × 16m and the upper storey, seen here, is entered by a door from a platform formed by the vaulted chambers beneath.

BELOW One of the massive corner towers of the keep of the citadel of Tartus, which is the largest surviving fortified structure in the city. It lies on the seafront and during the medieval period the shoreline lapped the foot of a small postern gate in the sloping talus. This is where the Templar garrison was believed to have escaped to on August 3, 1291, abandoning the last Crusader outpost on the Syrian mainland.

The island of Ru'ad lies a kilometre or so off the Syrian coast, near Tartus. A small castle overlooking the little harbour was constructed after the Crusaders were driven from the island in 1302, but another larger castle seen here lies almost hidden within the village that now covers Ru'ad. It is a simple, 13th-century, rectangular enclosure with rounded corner towers, yet it enabled a Templar garrison to hold the island for more than a decade after the fall of the last Crusader outposts on the mainland.

# Turkey

The northern regions of the Principality of Antioch included part of what is now the Turkish province of Antakya (also called the Hatay). Within this rugged territory the easiest Crusader fortifications to reach are the Citadel of Antioch (Antakya) itself and the castle of Bagras, which, though built by the Byzantines in AD 968, is largely Armenian and Crusader. Within the eastern part of the neighbouring Turkish province of Adana, Haruniya is more difficult to reach and is largely Islamic rather than Crusader, while Amoude, between Kozan and the great Cilician Armenian fortress of Toprakkale, only appears on the most detailed maps.

The citadel or upper fortifications of Antioch are almost entirely ruined, though some vaulted chambers from the Crusader castle remain. These were added to the Romano-Byzantine urban defences in the 12th and 13th centuries. They were destroyed when this, the capital of the Crusader Principality of Antioch, fell to the Mamluk Sultan Baybars in 1268. (Frederick Nicolle)

# Lebanon

The Crusader castles and fortified cities of Lebanon are accessible now that the civil war and Israeli occupation have ended. The citadel of Tripoli (Trablus) includes 12th–13th-century Crusader work, fragments of an 11th-century Islamic palace-fortress, and substantial Ottoman Turkish rebuilding. It is, however, in a good state of repair and well worth a visit. The same is true of Gibelet (Jbayl) and southern coastal cities like Sidon (Saida) and Tyre (Sur). In the very north of Lebanon the mountain castle of Gibelcar ('Akkar) remains difficult to reach, though this is a result of its dramatic location rather than any security considerations.

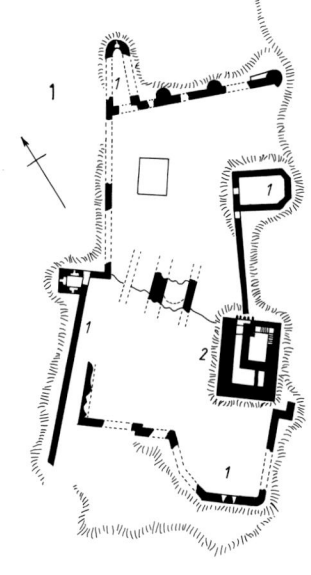

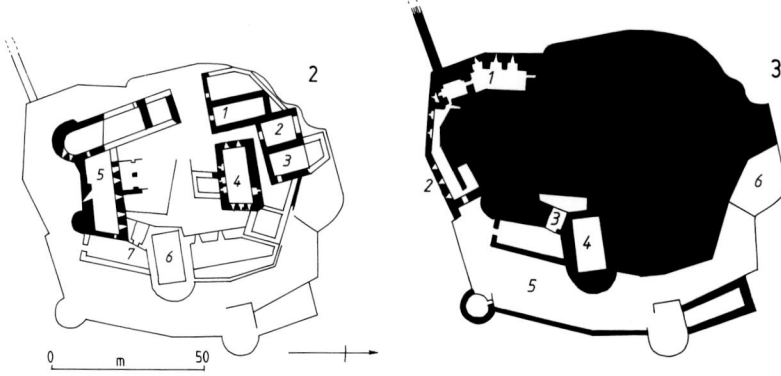

(1) The castle of Amoude:
1 – Armenian outer defences;
2 – donjon added by the Teutonic Knights in the 13th century. (After Edwards)

(2) Upper fortifications of the castle of Bagra (Baghras):
1–3 – magazine chambers;
4–5 – palatial residences;
6 – donjon;
7 – gatehouse from forecourt into upper castle. (After Müller-Wiener and Molin)

(3) Lower fortifications of the castle of Bagra (Baghras):
1–2 – lower galleries;
3 – gatehouse from forecourt into upper castle;
4 – donjon;
5–6 – bailey of the lower fortress. (After Müller-Wiener and Molin)

# Israel and the Palestinian Territories

Many castles and fortifications dating from the Crusader period have been excavated and restored within the state of Israel. Some almost resemble historical theme parks, but others have been treated more sympathetically. The Old City of Acre was one of the few Palestinian towns to retain is Arab population following the mass expulsions of 1948. This, when added to the skilful, sensitive and restrained manner in which Israeli archaeologists are still uncovering the ruins of the medieval city, makes Acre a top priority for those seeking Crusader fortifications in the Holy Land. Pilgrims' Castle at Atlit, south of Haifa, is still out of bounds because the location is currently used as a training base for Israeli Naval Commandos. However, the dramatic fortress is clearly visible from the coast. Southward again, the excavated site of Caesarea contains remarkable remains from many periods, of which the 13th-century Crusader fortifications are the best preserved. The equally remarkable but smaller and less known site of Arsuf lies on the coast just north of Herzliya. It was another closed military zone until a series of explosions and chemical leaks convinced the Israeli Defence Forces to move their weapons development facility from the site. Nevertheless, until the existing toxic pollution is removed, archaeological excavations and public access to the remains of medieval Arsuf will remain restricted.

# Further reading

Antaki, P. 'Le château Croisé de Beyrouth; étude préliminaire', *ARAM Periodical* 13/14 (2001/2) 323-353.

Avissar, M. & Stern, E. 'Akko, the Citadel,' *Excavations and Surveys in Israel*, XIV (1994) 22–25.

Biller, T. 'Der Crac des Chevaliers – neue Forschungen,' *Château Gaillard*, 20 (2002) 51–55.

Chevedden, P.E. 'Fortification and the Development of Defensive Planning in the Latin East,' in D. Kagay & L.J.A. Villalon (eds.), *The Circle of War in the Middle Ages* (Woodbridge 1999) 33–43.

Dean, B. 'A Crusader Fortress in Palestine (Montfort)', *Bulletin of the Metropolitan Museum of Art*, XXII/2 (1927) 91–97.

Deschamps, P. *Les Châteaux des Croisés en Terre Sainte: le Crac des Chevaliers* (Paris 1934).

Edbury, P.W. 'Castles, towns and rural settlements in the Crusader kingdom,' *Medieval Archaeology*, XLII (1998) 191–193.

Edwards, R.W. *The Fortifications of Armenian Cilicia* (Washington 1987).

Ellenblum, R. 'Frankish and Muslim Siege Warfare and the construction of Frankish concentric castles,' in M. Balard (ed.), *Die Gesta per Francos* (Aldershot 2001) 187–198.

Ellenblum, R. 'Three generations of Frankish castle-building in the Latin Kingdom of Jerusalem,' in M. Balard (ed.), *Autour de la Première Croisade* (Paris 1996) 517–551.

Eydoux, H-P. 'L'architecture militaire des Francs en Orient,' in J.P. Babelon (ed.), *Le Château en France* (Paris 1986) 61–77.

Faucherre, N. (et al eds.), *La Fortification au Temps des Croisades* (Rennes 2004).

Fedden, R. *Crusader castles: a brief study in the military architecture of the Crusades* (London 1950).

Folda, J. 'Crusaders Frescoes at Crac des Chevaliers and Marqab Castles,' *Dumbarton Oaks Papers*, XXXVI (1982) 177–210.

Fournet, T. 'Le château de Aakar al-Atiqa (Nord-Liban),' *Bulletin d'Archéologie et d'Architecture Libanaises*, 4 (2000) 149–163.

Gertwagen, R. 'The Crusader Port of Acre: Layout and Problems of Maintenance,' in M. Balard (ed.), *Autour de la Première Croisade* (Paris 1996) 553–582.

Hamma, Z. *Syria: The Castles and Archaeological Sites in Tartous (Governorate)* (Damascus 1994).

Hartal, M. 'Excavations of the Courthouse Site at 'Akko' (three parts) *'Atiqot* XXXI (1997) 1–2, 3–30, 109–114.

Jacoby, D. 'Crusader Acre in the Thirteenth Century; urban layout and topography,' *Studi Medievali*, 3 ser. XX (979) 1–45.

Jacoby, D. 'Montmussard, Suburb of Crusader Acre: The First Stages of its Development,' in *Outremer: Studies in the History of the Crusading Kingdom of Jerusalem presented to Joshua Prawer* (Jerusalem 1982) 205–217.

Jawish, H. *Krak des Chevaliers und die Kreuzfahrer* (Damascus 1999).

Johns, C.N. 'Excavations of Pilgrim's Castle, 'Atlit (1932-3): Stables at the south-west of the suburbs,' *Quarterly of the Department of Antiquities of Palestine*, V (1935) 31–60.

Kedar, B.Z. 'The Outer Walls of Frankish Acre,' *'Atiqot*, XXXI (1997) 157–180.

Kennedy, H. *Crusader Castles* (Cambridge 1994).

Marino, L. (ed.) *La fabbrica dei Castelli Crociati in Terra Santa* (Florence 1997).

Marino, L. The making of the Crusader Castels [sic.],' in L. Marino (ed), *La fabbrica dei castelli crociati in Terra Santa* (Florence 1997).

Mesqui, J. *Châteaux d'Orient, Liban, Syrie* (Paris 2001).

Molin, K. 'The non-military functions of Crusader fortifications, 1187–circa 1380,' *Journal of Medieval History*, XXIII (1997) 367–388.

Molin, K. *Unknown Crusader Castles* (London 2001).

Müller-Wiener, W. *Castles of the Crusaders* (London 1966).

Nordiguian, L. and Voisin, J-C. *Châteaux et églises du moyen âge au Liban* (Beirut 1999).

Pringle, D. 'A Thirteenth Century Hall at Montfort Castle in Western Galilee,' *The Antiquaries Journal*, LXVI (1986) 52–81.

Pringle, D. 'Architecture in the Latin East', in Riley-Smith, J.S.C. (ed), *Oxford Illustrated History of the Crusades* (Oxford 1995) 160–183.

Pringle, D. 'Reconstructing the Castle of Safad,' *Palestine Exploration Quarterly*, CXVII (1985) 139–149.

Pringle, D., 'The Castle and Lordship of Mirabel,' in Kedar, B.Z. (ed) *Montjoie – Studies in Crusader history in Honour of Hans Eberhard Mayer* (Aldershot 1997) 91–112.

Pringle, D. 'Towers in Crusader Palestine,' *Château Gaillard 1992*, XVI (Caen 1994) 335–370.

Pringle, D. 'Town Defences in the Crusader Kingdom of Jerusalem,' in Corfis, I.A. and Wolfe, M. (eds.) *The Medieval City under Siege* (Woodbridge 1995) 69–121.

Pringle, D. *Fortification and Settlement in Crusader Palestine* (reprints, Aldershot 2000).

Pringle, D. *Secular Buildings in the Crusader Kingdom of Jerusalem; An Archaeological Gazetteer* (Cambridge 1997).

Pringle, D. *The Red Tower (al Burj al Ahmar): Settlement on the Plain of Sharon at the time of the Crusades and Mamluks ...* (British School of Archaeology Monographs, Series 1) (London 1986).

Rihaoui, A. *The Krak of the Knights* (Damascus 1996).

Riley-Smith, J. 'The Templars and the castle of Tortosa in Syria; an unknown document concerning the acquisition of the fortress,' *English Historical Review*, LXXXIV (1969) 278–288.

Roll, I. 'Medieval Apollonia – Arsuf; A Fortified Coastal Town in the Levant of the Early Muslim and Crusader Periods,' in M. Balard (ed.), *Autour de la Première Croisade* (Paris 1996) 595–606.

# Glossary

**ablaq**  Middle Eastern tradition of architectural decoration combining different coloured stone

**antemurabilus**  second or outer walls

**ashlar**  stone cut into rectangular blocks and laid in regular rows

**bailey, bailli**  fortified enclosure with a castle

**barbican**  outer defensive enclosure, usually outside a gate

**barrel vault**  vaulting in the form of an elongated arch

**bastion**  projecting or additional part of a fortification

**castrum** (pl. **castra**)  fortified enclosure, usually rectangular

**châtelain**  commander of a castle

**chemin de ronde**  raised walkway around the circuit or curtain-walls

**concentric castle**  fortification with two or more circuit walls

**corbel**  stone bracket to support another structure

**crenellation**  tooth-like projections along the top of a fortified wall to provide protection for the defenders

**cubit**  unclear unit of measure, about half a metre

**curtain wall**  continuous defensive wall around a fortified location

**donjon**  main tower of a fortified location, or a single isolated tower

**double-castrum**  fortified enclosure with two concentric defensive walls

**drawbridge**  entrance bridge, usually over a moat, which can be raised, usually blocking the gate behind

**embossed masonry**  blocks of stone in which the centre is raised and usually roughly cut

**embrasure**  opening in a fortified wall through which the defenders can shoot

**enceinte**  curtain-wall

**forewalls**  additional defensive walls in front of the main defensive walls and towers

**fosse**  defensive ditch

**galleries**  passages, usually within a defensive wall, sometimes with embrasures

**glacis**  smooth slope leading to the base of a fortified wall

**hoarding**  wooden structure in the form of a gallery mounted on top of, and also ahead of, a defensive wall

**keep**  main tower of a fortified position (see *donjon*)

**machicolation**  overhanging structure on a tower or fortified wall

**merlons**  raised masonry forming a crenellation (see above)

**moat**  ditch or fosse forming an obstruction outside a defensive wall

**motte and bailey**  castle consisting of a tower on a small man-made hill (*motte*), with an outer fortified enclosure (*bailey*)

**portcullis**  grid-like gate or iron or iron and wood, usually raised an lower into position inside a gateway

**posterns**  small doors or gates in the defences of a fortified position

**redoubt**  outwork of a fortified place

**salient towers**  towers thrust forwards from a fortified wall

**slot machicolation**  aperture above a broad groove down the face of a tower or fortified wall

**spur-castle**  castle built on a spur or promontory, usually on the side of a hill

**talus**  additional sloping front along the lower part of a wall and tower

**undercroft**  lowest chamber of a multi-storey building or structure

**ward**  open area surrounded by a curtain wall

# Index

Figures in **bold** refer to illustrations